The world is fu... book records i... happenings from ...g ...l ...rious English-speaking countries. Read about the man at the smart San Francisco hotel who literally launders the money of the super rich. Or the car thief, Mr Wideawake, who was arrested whilst asleep in his stolen vehicle . . .

Contents

With grateful thanks for their help to Angela Needs; Tim Pace; Clive Cohen; Rick Turner; Ian Hook; and our Parents

What is life's purpose and value?

A 24-year-old Chinese medical student who died when he dived into a vat of human excrement, in an attempt to save an old peasant who had fallen in, has become a national hero for his devotion to duty. Chinese newspapers have been devoting full pages to the diaries, photos and school reports of Zhang Hua, the deceased student, who succumbed to methane gas fumes arising from the human waste, which was being stored in the vat until it decomposed and could be used in the fields. Chinese officials hope that he will be a model for others. Says Zhang Shaoxue, President of the Student Ethics Society of the Chinese People's University: 'Zhang Hua has provided an answer to what we've been discussing and thinking about: "What is life's purpose and value?"'
(*Toronto Globe & Mail*)

A Staffordshire Fire Station is to be reported to the Health and Safety Executive because the Fire Brigade's Union claims it is a fire risk. Eccleshall Fire Station dates back to the 1880s and houses one 1972 fire engine. 'The only reason the fire engine actually fits the building is that it's not a modern one,' says Stafford Fire Brigade Union Chairman, Mr Terry Brown. 'The water runs in down the walls where there are electric fires and plugs. That constitutes a fire risk,' he adds. The sum of £116,000 is required to modernise the station, so for the time being

1

the firemen will have to endure the snails and slugs which inhabit the building, as well as the possibility of returning from a job to see a pile of charred rubble. (*The Guardian*)

A bomb-sniffing dog was demoted by the Air Force after he failed to tell the difference between a bomb and dirty underwear, resulting in the detonation of a suitcase containing a sergeant's grubby smalls. It smelled pretty explosive to Napoleon, a 5-year-old mutt, and so he singled the case out. The bomb squad was summoned. His superiors at Dyess Air Force Base in Abilene, Texas, moved him on to other duties. ('P.D.', St Louis Post-Dispatch)

According to the Soviet newspaper *Izvestia*, Russian sociologists estimate that boorish and rude behaviour towards comrade workers consumes about an hour and fifteen minutes of each eight-hour working day. 'For an hour and a quarter,' says *Izvestia* writer Nadezhda Kolovkova, 'people scream at one another, take tranquillisers, sulk, or stare into space re-experiencing offences.' She asks, 'Isn't this a bit much for emotion?' (*Izvestia*, in *World Press Review*)

Eighty-four workers with the US Public Health Service in Washington are being moved to other quarters because their present offices are suspected of being a health hazard. Public Health workers in one area of the Hubert H. Humphrey Building have reported aches, fevers, chills and nausea, which seemed to disappear at weekends. Leaks of greasy water from a cafeteria above are suspected of spreading bacteria. (*Los Angeles Times*)

Washington State representative Lois Stratton received a polite reception to the campaign speech she delivered to a Spokane gathering of the American Association of Retired

2

Persons. The applause wasn't thunderous, but it wasn't too bad, considering that the candidate was addressing the wrong crowd. She was supposed to be speaking down the hall to the Retired Public Employees. (Los Angeles Times)

An Essex cashier who admitted stealing £700 from her employer was granted a conditional discharge by a London court; magistrate John Nichols showed mercy towards 56-year-old Eileen Hall after he was told that, after twenty-three years with the company, she was making just £40 a week. He called that 'extraordinary'. (*Daily Telegraph*)

Should the US Army pay $309,400 to teach female recruits at Fort Jackson, South Carolina how to apply make-up? Fort Jackson's procurement chief, Thomas Cooper, has his doubts. He expected that $20,000 would be a fair price when he let out word that bids were being accepted for the make-up instruction. But the only bid received was from the University of South Carolina's Centre for Lifelong Learning in nearby Columbia. Apparently expecting to hop on the military spending gravy train, they quoted a price of $309,400. Cooper thinks he'll tell them to take a powder, and will look for 'an alternative route'. (*San Diego Union* AP)

A Swedish Defence spokesman, Major Borje Johansson, is suggesting that disco music may be to blame for the failure of young navy personnel to locate an alien submarine in Hors Bay. The Major thinks that loud disco music has damaged the young sailors' hearing to the point that they are unable to hear the sub's tell-tale beeps. (Los Angeles Times)

3

The status and pay of Chinese intellectuals needs to be upgraded, says the newspaper *China Daily*. It complains that college students in China earn more than their professors do, when food allowances are included. (*Miami Herald*)

An increasing number of people turning to a Beverly Hills, California security firm for protection are requesting female bodyguards. As a result, Herman Marx, who owns 'Personal Protection Service', has added five women to his staff. Marx says his requests for women bodyguards come from other women, as well as from men who don't want their protection to be too conspicuous. This way, a man can avoid social embarrassment by simply introducing the woman as his live-in lover. But, says Marx 'when the occasion arises, I can guarantee you they can handle themselves'. (*San Francisco Chronicle*)

Live broadcasts of parliamentary debates in the House of Commons have made the House sound 'like a second-rate beer hall', according to a report by a House Committee which surveyed Members. The Members were particularly troubled by the level of background noise while the crucial issues of the day were being discussed. Rather than tackle the impossible task of getting legislators to pipe down, the committee reported it is investigating 'technical means' of reducing noise from the background on broadcasts. (Daily Telegraph)

The very special people who can afford the very special room rates at San Francisco's posh St Francis Hotel can utilise a very special service the hotel offers free of charge – having their money laundered at the hotel's money laundry. At least, that applies to coins. The coin-cleaning service supposedly began to keep dirty coins from soiling the ladies' white gloves. The current coin-washer is 78-

year-old Arnold Batliner. He says: 'They tell me I've washed $11 million in coins since 1962.' He uses a silver-burnishing machine that can handle over $4,000 in pennies, nickels, dimes and quarters at once. Batliner says: 'The pennies are the hardest to clean.' (*Portland Oregonian*)

Discussion of the problem of drug and alcohol abuse in sports took a new twist at a meeting of the International Federation of University Sport in Edmonton, Canada. The Federation voted to institute, at the next World University Games, compulsory testing of volleyball referees for drunkenness. Federation General Secretary Roch Campana of Belgium said the time had come to blow the whistle on inebriated officials because of incidents where they were so drunk they 'couldn't blow the whistle decently'. (*Vancouver Sun*)

A member of the House of Lords has suggested that the National Health Service should treat whisky as a prescription drug, and pay for such prescriptions. It was 98-year-old Lord Shinwell who noted that most doctors agree on the medicinal properties of whisky, and that treating it as medicine 'would help many of us who depend on that kind of medicine'. (Daily Telegraph)

In Belgrade, Yugoslavia, the newspaper *Politika* reports the arrests of two workers whose on-the-job drinking not only sent their own heads spinning, but those of others as well. The men got drunk while operating a merry-go-round, and sent it spinning around so fast that it collapsed, injuring six riders. They then headed off for some more rounds at a bar, where they were arrested. (*Los Angeles Times*)

5

Democracy in action was an enriching experience for Indonesians in that country's recent national elections. Each person attending a campaign rally of the ruling Golkar party received $9. That's ten times the minimum daily wage. Golkar's chief opponent, the United Development ment Party, offered somewhat less. They lost. (*Christian Science Monitor*)

Britain's Royal Philharmonic Orchestra is winning an appreciative new audience by taking its offerings into factories for lunch-time concerts, as part of a programme by the Greater London Council to spread high culture around. Car workers at the Dagenham Ford plant responded enthusiastically to appropriate selections from 'Carmen'. So loudly did the crowd gathered in the factory's lunchroom stamp and cheer and clap that the beaming conductor, Harry Rabinowitz, turned around and started conducting the audience. The concert cost taxpayers £5,000 but most of the workers agreed it was a worthwhile break from the usual factory sounds of heavy metal. (Daily Telegraph)

There are a lot more queens at Buckingham Palace than most people ever suspected, according to Britain's *Sun* newspaper. The paper quotes a member of the Palace staff as saying that up to 100 of the 300 Palace employees are gay. (*Chicago Tribune*)

Feminists in Russia still have a long way to go, too. The publication *Woman and Russia*, produced by the country's Leningrad-based feminist movement, complained that Soviet men are irresponsible drunkards and that Soviet society 'degrades women to the status of a work animal, a sex object and a breeding machine'. Now a founder of the movement, 35-year-old Natalya Lazareva, has been sentenced to four years in prison and a further two years of internal exile for 'slandering the Soviet state and social system'. She could have been imprisoned for seven years, but, according to the *Tass* News Agency, she showed 'sincere repentance'. (*Daily Telegraph*)

A drop in milk production among Soviet cows may be because farmhands swear at them too much, a scientific worker suggests in the Russian newspaper Rural Life. *T. Dmitrieva, of the All-Russian Scientific Methodology Centre, writes: 'Cows that are cursed at give less milk,' which, of course, only leads to more cursing, which becomes a vicious cycle resulting in udder failure.* (Los Angeles Times)

British poet Adrian Mitchell is willing to forego the lucrative schoolbook business in order to stick to his poetic principles. In a preface to his book *Collected Poems – 1953 to 1979* to be published later this month, Mitchell stipulates that teachers must not use his poems for examinations. He says that poems should be used for 'joy and fun', and not as 'a way of getting a certificate to get a job'. Mitchell says he doesn't want to end up like 'poor old Wordsworth', hated by children forced to memorise his verse. (*Daily Telegraph*)

When police in Zambia are called about a crime taking place, their response is often: 'We have no transport, can you come and pick us up?' (*New York Times*)

The Los Angeles County Sheriff's Department is using sex to lure new recruits who read Playboy *magazine. The department reports an excellent response to its* Playboy *ad that shows a white page covered with lush, red lipstick prints, and the message: 'Be someone's hero.'* Playboy *provided the ad free of charge, as have other publications solicited by the department for free ad space.*

7

Another ad in some local magazines features a view of the Sunset Strip and the words: 'Cruise Sunset, we'll pay for the gas.' (San Diego Union)

Energy Secretary James B. Edwards told a press conference in Richland, Washington: 'I think the future of nuclear energy is a glowing future.' (*Washington Post*)

The commercial for Brazilian coffee was not the Australian broadcasting tribunal's cup of tea. It's banned the TV ad, on the grounds that the man delivering the testimonial for Brazilian coffee is a real bad actor, convicted 'Great Train Robber' Ronald Biggs, who later escaped from a British prison and now resides beyond the reach of British justice in Rio de Janeiro. The ad shows Biggs sipping a cup on an apartment balcony, and saying: 'When you're on the run all the time like me, you really appreciate a good cup of coffee.' And, he says, the price is a 'real steal'. (*Los Angeles Times*)

Country singer Stella Parton says she switched over from gospel music because she couldn't make ends meet in gospel, even though she was on the big-time circuit. The problem, says Parton, was cheating gospel promoters. She says: 'There are bigger crooks in the gospel business than you'll ever find in country music. That just broke my heart.' (Music Connection)

The *Los Angeles Times* offers a good explanation for why fresh fish is so hard to find in Russia. Apparently, in Russia's Baltic seaports, fishing trawlers have to wait up to three weeks to unload their catches. (*Los Angeles Times*)

Drug abuse in the military is related to a shortage of ammunition, South Carolina Senator Ernest Hollings recently suggested. He was speaking for a measure he was sponsoring to appropriate $148 million for extra ammo for the Army. Said Hollings: 'There is no man happier than a 19- or 20-year-old when he is firing his weapon.' The measure was defeated. (*Boston Globe*)

According to a survey by the Italian Communist Party newspaper L'Unita, *87 per cent of shopkeepers in Naples pay protection money to Mafia-style gangs.* (Portland Oregonian)

You wouldn't know you were in China if you visited the town of Shenzhen. It's one of four special economic zones where Chinese officials are allowing capitalism to flourish, as an experiment in development, and a way to build up China's export potential and attract money from Hong Kong. Big cars crowd the streets, along with long-haired motor-cycle gangs, teenagers in skin-tight Levis work electronic games, and prostitutes ply their trade, in the shadow of skyscrapers that are going up. Wages are much higher than in the rest of China, and everybody has access to the racy television signals of nearby Hong Kong. So, how ya gonna keep 'em down on the commune, after they've seen Shenzhen? Easy. The Chinese are spending $70 million to erect a high barbed-wire-topped fence around the town. (*Washington Post*)

The 160-member 'Flying Funeral Directors Association' is grieving over a US Federal Aviation Administration ruling that the cadavers they transport in their planes are considered passengers. That means they must meet the much stiffer requirements and rules for commercial pilots, rather than being able to fly as private pilots. And it means much stiffer insurance rates. Says an FAA spokesman: 'A passenger is a passenger.' The Association, however, is refusing to roll over and play dead. A Federal

9

Court in Philadelphia is to hear their appeal. (*Washington Post*)

The call of the kestrel hawk may soon echo through Westminster Abbey. *Abbey officials have put out their own call for a recording of the hawk's call. They want to play it to scare off pigeons who have taken up residence in the rafters and leave daily offerings on the high altar. Says one official, Geoffrey Day: 'We don't want to bring in marksmen with air guns and gas canisters at this stage.'* (Sunday Times)

A 64-page magazine on conserving resources has been released by the Illinois Department of Energy and Natural Resources, with nine of the pages blank. It's a waste of paper, but, on the positive side, it shows how ink can be conserved. (*Chicago Tribune*)

Television has been accused of anaesthetising the nation's young, and now a New York orthodontist is putting that to good use. Dr Marc Lemchen is anaesthetising his patients with TV sets placed around the dental chairs. The kids view videotaped shows while their mouths are being worked on, and Dr Lemchen says: 'Kids are so enthralled watching television that they're totally oblivious to discomfort.' (*San Francisco Chronicle*)

Quote of the day, from Henry Kissinger: 'The nice thing about being a celebrity is that when you bore people, they think it's their fault.' (*Herb Caen*, San Francisco Chronicle)

Who says there are no jobs available? The Thruway Sewer & Drain Service Co. of New York says sewer-cleaner jobs are going begging, even though the firm pays above the minimum wage. Says a spokesperson: 'A lot of people look down on sewer cleaning.' (*Wall Street Journal*)

Firefighters used oxygen masks to revive about 360 pigs after a fire broke out at the Midland Pig Unit in Softon, England. The pigs had been felled by smoke inhalation. But another 300-odd pigs were too far gone to be revived, and became smoked bacon. (*Daily Telegraph*)

Reason *magazine reports that the Equal Employment Opportunity Commission has reviewed some 150 cases in which people claimed to have been discriminated against in jobs because they were vampires, or suspected of such. Often their birthplace – Transylvania – seems to have been enough to arouse the employer's suspicions.* (Reason)

There's a big sign up in the Huntington, West Virginia shop of sign painter Carl Workman. It says: 'All political work must be paid in advance.' Workman, who does a lot of work for politicians during election years, has learned from experience how far they can be trusted. He says: 'If they get beat in the primary, you have a hard time getting your money.' (*Los Angeles Times*)

US Senator Paul E. Tsongas of Massachusetts told a conference of business people in Boston: 'The evidence of Japanese penetration of US markets is all too obvious.' He said that it's time for Americans to come to grips with the problem. Actually, Tsongas couldn't be there in person, but he sent along a speech recorded on a *Sony* videocassette, and driven to the airport in a *Toyota*. (*Miami Herald*)

The bullet-riddled bodies of four undertakers were found in a car in Caserta, Italy. Police feel this may be part of a deadly war for control of the Naples funeral business. (The Times)

The Chairman of the Greater London Council's Transport Committee led a protest against a higher body's decision to double public transport fares in London. David Wetzel boarded a bus and refused to pay more than the old fare. When the bus driver ordered him off, Wetzel turned to his fellow passengers and asked them to vote on whether he should stay on the bus. They voted for him to get off. (*The Times*)

Father Anton Wagner was a consummate art collector. Police in Augsburg, West Germany, were impressed. They seized 3,000 stolen works of art, worth around £150,000, from the priest's four homes in Augsburg. He was charged with stealing the art from churches, homes, schools and stores. Father Wagner told authorities: 'You would not believe how many presents a priest gets.' He was right. (*The Guardian*)

Gustave Jansson, the Michigan prison inmate who billed himself as 'Your Honest Con', has dropped out of the race for governor. The 34-year-old convicted sex offender has thrown his support behind Lt Gov. James Brickley. Meanwhile, the campaign of another candidate for Michigan governor got off to a bad start when his mother came out against him. James Weller, a 33-year-old lawyer, lives at home. Said his mother Mary Weller: 'Any campaign he runs would be a total failure.' (Los Angeles Times, Sacramento Bee)

Teachers at the Avery Elementary School in Buena Vista, Colorado, were told to come up with a study list of words, in preparation for a spelling test to be held there. According to Principal Jerry Parsons, among the words the teachers produced were 'humerous', 'brillient', 'feable', 'formorly' and 'bookeeping'. Fortunately, the misspelled words were spotted by students and parents. Said

12

Principal Parsons: 'I don't no what to say.' (*Denver Post, Sacramento Bee*)

Are you desperate enough for a job that you'd work as a human lavatory? Some public servants in medieval Britain did just that. They'd roam the streets wearing a huge cape and carrying a pail. Patrons using the pail in this portable toilet would have their privacy ensured when the worker spread his cape. This titbit is one of many pungent bits dropped by Colin Lucas in a new book detailing the history of the lavatory, entitled *Hygiene in the Buildings* (published by Rentokil in Britain). Lucas also tells the amusing tale of Richard the Raker, a latrine cleaner who fell through the floor and drowned in excrement. (*The Times*)

In London, Ontario, 41-year-old Cletus Dore wants a job so badly that he placed a classified ad in the London Free Press, offering a $500 reward to anyone who hires him. He says he doesn't have the money now, but will once the pay cheques start rolling in. (Vancouver Sun)

Mr Bhandara has a bit of a marketing problem. He's Chief Executive of the Murree Brewery Company in Rawalpindi, Pakistan. They've been in the business since 1861, but sales have dropped since Pakistani authorities announced five years ago that any Moslem found with alcohol would face the whip, fines, and imprisonment. Moslems make up 97 per cent of the population. Non-Moslem Pakistanis can still imbibe, but only on festive religious occasions. A plea by Buddhists that, for them, every day is a religious festival, has not been warmly received. Foreigners can still drink, but Mr Bhandara has a marketing problem – there's only one bar in the entire country. And, to make matters worse, there's a total ban on exports. In case the brewery tries to get sneaky,

13

Pakistani President Zia has his office just across the street. He rents it from the brewery. But Mr Bhandara is cheerfully philosophical, in keeping with the Murree Brewery slogan: 'Eat, drink and be Murree.' He says: 'There have been many ups and downs in the fortunes of this company . . . we will be back.' In the meanwhile, they've diversified into fruit juice. (*Daily Telegraph*)

A St Albans dry cleaning firm advertises: 'Our guarantee: should you feel we have failed you in any way, we will be only too pleased to do it again at no extra charge.' (*Daily Telegraph*)

Results of the biscuit-baking contest at the County Fair in San Diego proved that, at least in California, sex roles aren't what they used to be. When the tasting was over, boys had walked off with the top spots for best-biscuit recipe in all five age groups. (Los Angeles Daily News)

The University of Florida's Committee on the Care and Use of Laboratory Animals has voted 9–1 to proceed with cocaine experiments using monkeys and birds. The vote rejected the pleas of 258 student animal rights supporters who volunteered to be human guinea pigs in the cocaine studies. (*Miami Herald*)

In Millbrook, Alabama, police officer James Owens and dispatcher Nancy Dunn have been fired, after neighbours who saw a house burning got no answer when they phoned the fire station. They then drove there, and reported that the two were 'standing there watching the (lunar) eclipse'. The two denied the allegations. (*San Francisco Chronicle*)

It was quite a snappy April Fool's joke played on workers at the Draper-King Cole Cannery *in Milton, Delaware.*

14

Workers unloading a crate of green beans found a 4-foot 9-in alligator among the beans. It was definitely alive, said William P. Dellinger. He can vouch for that, he said, 'since I had to hold the mouth shut'. (San Diego Union)

The effort you put out comes back to you, 18-year-old Stephen Roe demonstrated. The Doncaster youth rebounded from unemployment when a company was so impressed with his work on a government-financed programme that it hired him full-time for his specialty – carving boomerangs. (*The Guardian*)

Future wars between nations may be conducted by computers against other computers, says computer-security analyst Donn B. Parker. He told a conference in Monte Carlo that he foresees the threat of nuclear war being replaced by economic holocaust, with computers invading and sabotaging enemy computers. They would wreck commodities markets by manipulating weather forecasts, could alter enemy computer files controlling the distribution of energy, and could foul up the electronic funds transfer network. (*Science News*)

A news crew from a TV station in Trenton, New Jersey showed up at Trenton City Hall to do a special feature on the city's innovative 'workfare' programme. Under the programme, twenty social security recipients work four days a month each as security guards at City Hall. But the news crew was not impressed by what they saw. None of the five recipients scheduled for duty that day had shown up. One phoned in with back problems, one was late arriving, and no explanations were available for the absences of the other three. (Washington Post)

Reporters are being sought for one of the toughest journalism jobs around – working for the *San Quentin*

15

News, a weekly that goes out to the 3,000 inmates of the California prison. Though the weekly was recently judged best prison newspaper in a contest sponsored by the Southern Illinois University School of Journalism, good reporters are hard to hang onto. Reporters burn out quickly, says Staff Photographer, Jimmy Price, because they have to walk a tightrope. They can't offend prison authorities too much, and, on the other hand, they don't want to offend any of their readers, who can reply with sharp retorts not confined to the letters-to-the-editor page. (*Miami Herald*)

Practically every activity seems to run the risk of some type of injury, and now that appears to apply even to sitting still. According to *Working Woman* magazine, sitting or standing for too long in one place can produce a swelling of the feet and ankles known as 'pedal oedema'. Blood collects in the lower extremities because the person's lack of muscular activity makes it harder to return it to the heart. The best treatment is movement, but if that's too demanding, then at least raise your legs. (*Working Woman*)

The jobs which produce the most stress-related illnesses are those which have the least worries, according to a study by the University of Michigan Institute for Social Research. For instance, assembly line workers, who reported the greatest boredom, had the highest levels of anxiety and physical disorders. Jobs with the most responsibility, on the other hand, caused the least psychosomatic illness. (Family Weekly)

God accomplished a miracle today

CONGRATULATIONS to 35-year-old Lloyd Lummis of the Vancouver suburb of Burnaby, who's just crossed Canada on foot – crossed Canada in more than one way. He made the 4,600-mile walk carrying a 14 ft × 18 ft wooden cross. 'God accomplished a miracle today,' he said as he arrived in Corner Brook, Newfoundland. The Lord aside, he was helped with his burden by a wheel attached to the base of the cross. It took him three years, as he made stops by the wayside to make friends, get married and have a baby. (*Vancouver Sun*)

A man in County Tyrone, N. Ireland, who tried to fiddle his electricity meter, turned the key the wrong way and got a bill for £600 – ten times the normal amount. He was taken to court and fined £25 for his trouble. (*Australian Age*)

A German artist who pushed a machine dripping pig's blood from Kassel to London claims to have created the longest work of art in the world. The machine, which is normally used to mark boundaries on sports fields, was filled with pig's blood supplied by a network of abattoirs en route. Artist Gunther Demnig arrived at British Customs only to find that officials considered his machine to have infringed import regulations. This matter overcome, Demnig triumphantly arrived at London's Tate

17

Gallery and left the machine there overnight. When he returned in the morning he found that the brake blocks and cables with which he had equipped his machine had been stolen. (London Event)

Warden George Sumner of the Nevada State Prison in Carson City says that people have drawn the wrong impression from news that three inmates were found to have built an almost-completed helicopter in the prison. Says the warden, 'They just wanted to see if it could fly. They didn't want to use it for an escape.' He says past prison administrators had been aware of their little hobby, but took no action. Nevertheless, the three are to be charged with possession of contraband and misuse of State property. (*Nevada State Journal*)

They put up overhead street lights in the Umoja housing estate on the outskirts of Nairobi, Kenya, in order to cut down on the number of night-time burglaries in the area. Now, the Kenyan News Agency reports that half the newly installed lights have been stolen. (*Los Angeles Times*)

Police in Noblesville, Indiana, say that Hiram S. Edens stole a diamond ring from the home of Barbara Turner so he could present it to a young woman he was trying to impress. She wasn't very favourably impressed, though — it was her mother's ring. Edens was arrested. (Los Angeles Daily News)

Fulton County police in Georgia stopped a car driven by 21-year-old James William Estes Jr of Roswell, and charged him with a nude burglary and an attempted nude burglary at an apartment complex. Estes allegedly first removed his clothes at a Dunkin Donuts store, before heading out on his crimes. He was charged with indecent exposure, burglary, attempted burglary, being a Peeping Tom, public indecency, driving under the influence and improper lane use. (*Atlanta Journal*)

Having absolutely the messiest, grungiest kitchen will be worth a $500 gift certificate for someone in the Vancouver area. IDEA Furniture of suburban Richmond is holding an 'Ugliest Kitchen' photo contest. Says the store's marketing manager Len Laycock: 'We're looking for the ugliest, slimiest, cruddiest kitchen.' (*Vancouver Sun*)

The question is: how many riders are required on each elephant during a game of elephant polo? The answer, at least according to the way the game is played in Nepal, is three. The player sits on the elephant's back while the beast is manoeuvred around by two drivers – one on the elephant's neck and the other standing at the back. People on this side of the water may soon have a chance to upstage the horsey set, because a World Elephant Polo Association has just been formed. (Sunday Express)

Leon Kaplan says, 'I'd like to stand up for American cars.' The Los Angeles inventor is, in fact, preparing to go through hell and high water on their behalf. Next summer he plans to drive 4,000 miles to Japan, taking the most direct driving route across the Pacific Ocean, to make his stand. He's building his special car for the trip right now, out of Chrysler, General Motors and Ford parts. He calls it the 'All-American Special'. The car would be strapped to special hulls, with its wheels pushing roller tracks to turn hydraulic gears linked to a propeller. The steering wheel will be linked to a rudder. (*San Francisco Chronicle*)

Five cattle who took up residence on the top floor of a dilapidated house near Bellingham, Washington, were finally sweet-talked into leaving, with the aid of an offering of hay, by Herman Henspeters. Henspeters, a retired janitor who was looking after the property in the owner's absence, says that two bulls and two yearlings apparently followed a heifer in heat into the house and upstairs. The ensuing party saw some walls knocked down and floors carpeted with manure. (*Portland Oregonian*)

President Reagan discussed White House preparations for a nuclear holocaust at the annual dinner of the White House Correspondents' Association. He told the assembled: 'On the way in here tonight, someone handed me a question that said: "What is the White House doing to lessen the threat of being caught in a nuclear holocaust?" Well, I can assure you, we thought of that. We're putting in a smoke alarm.' The President was joking. (Chicago Tribune)

Parents of marriageable daughters in India's Bihar state are giving new meaning to the term 'shotgun wedding'. Because of soaring dowry demands which can be as high as £24,000 for professional men, many parents have simply started hiring armed gangs to kidnap the grooms of their choice, who then wed at gunpoint. Local officials say that there have been at least 500 cases of this in the past two months. Weddings are popular abduction spots, since they're full of eligible bachelors. The situation has become so serious that many parents won't allow their sons to go out alone, or else hire armed bodyguards for them. Curiously, though, the kidnapped grooms usually end up reconciling themselves to the marriage – divorce is very uncommon among Hindus. (*The Guardian*)

20

A lovesick swan with a crush on model boats has been responsible this spring for the sinking of three such boats and damage to two others at his lake abode in Batley, Yorkshire. It's happened each spring since George the swan lost his second mate three years ago. With the onset of mating season, George's romantic attentions turn to the model boats, which he races towards and embraces in a passionate flapping of wings and splashing of webbed feet. Or he'll gently nuzzle the boats and feed them grass. George's perversion has cost model boat hobbyists who use the lake over £400 in damages so far this year. (*Sunday Express*)

The Miami area's art conscious metro commission has found a place for Dutch sculptor Karel Appel's $44,195 aluminium tulip. It now adorns the mounds of rubbish at a municipal garbage-dumping and transfer facility. A metro ordinance requires that 1.5 per cent of the cost of public structures be spent on art. Garbage truck drivers generally like the aluminium tulip. In the words of Miami driver Robert Williams, it adds a little class. (Miami Herald)

London TV shop sales manager Michael Stoupas had a unique line to lay on Jayne Miskin, a young beauty consultant who walked by his store every day. One day he went up to her and told her that every time she walked by, all his display sets went on the blink. The answer lay with her breasts, as she discovered. It was her bra. Manufacturer George Callipulous admitted that he'd been using surplus electronic wire for the cups on 10,000 bras. This discovery turned into uplifting news for thousands of British TV viewers who had been plagued with bad reception. It was apparently the combination of body heat and movement of the wire's covering that had produced static electrical interference. (*Globe*)

In Miami, US District Court judge Joe Eaton has ruled that a Rabbi who can't go to a synagogue because of ill health has the right to pray at home, despite Council Bylaws. Miami beach officials had tried to prosecute Rabbi Naftali Grosz for zoning violations, because he prayed in a small building behind his house, along with nine other men required to complete a Jewish prayer quorum. Miami beach officials, maintaining that group prayer is a council violation, say they'll appeal. The day after the court decision, however, they granted a noted local resident, Saudi Arabian Sheik Mohammed Al-Fassi, the right to pray on his estate, as long as only members of his immediate family join him in prayer. They approved a building permit for the sheik to build a $75,000 mosque on his property. (*Miami Herald*)

The internal revenue service has filed a lien against the West Farmington, Ohio, property of Roy Elza, over an unpaid tax bill. Elza owes 18¢. (Chicago Tribune)

Lawyer Harry Ryan III told jurors in Rutland, Vermont, that he twice drove his car up and down the steps of the local jail in order to cheer up his client, whom the lawyer was delivering to the jail to begin a 31-month sentence. Unamused jurors fined him $100 and ordered his licence taken away for thirty days. (*Los Angeles Times*)

California cities cannot ban teenage car-cruising up and down their streets, the State Court of Appeals has ruled. The court overturned two tickets which Michael David Aguilar received from the town of Los Gatos. Aguilar ran foul of an ordinance prohibiting cruising in downtown Los Gatos, with cruising being defined as driving 'without immediate destination, at random, but on the look-out for possible developments or for the purposes of sightseeing repeatedly in the same area'. Aguilar's lawyers, including attorneys from the American Civil Liberties Union, argued that the State Vehicle Code prohibits local governments from passing such laws. (*San Francisco Chronicle*)

Sheriff's deputies were summoned to an Entiat, Washington, laundrette by a woman who complained that a man had removed all his clothes to wash them. But they decided to take no action after the man explained that he was from Quebec, and that's how they do things in Quebec. (*Wenatchee (Wash.) World, in* New Yorker)

The lucky inhabitants of eighty luxury apartments in a new New York highrise block will enjoy a breathtaking view from their balconies – a cityscape of awesome skyscrapers and quaint brownstone buildings. This luxurious view will be painted on the 27-floor-high brick wall that faces the balconies, 20 feet away. Rose Associates, the apartments' developers, are paying muralist Jeff Greene $100,000 to produce the city scene on the wall. Greene says: 'We'll use colours that we hope will bounce right back into the units.' (*New Yorker* magazine)

Chinese Government authorities have launched a crackdown on foreign music cassettes deemed 'pornographic'. Objectionable tapes are being seized from stores. According to *Billboard* magazine, high on the list of objectionable music are middle-of-the-road love ballads. Not that they care for disco either. (*Billboard*)

15-year-old Peter Fisher has been sent home from the Mosslands Boys School in Wallasey, England, because of his hair length. He's been told he'll only be re-admitted to class when his hair is at a proper length, which means it will have to cover his ears. His new military-style haircut offended headmaster William Mitchel, who told him it looked 'stupid', was a disgrace, and that he'd have to grow his sideburns back. Peter's mother, Rita Fisher, stuck up for her delinquent son, saying: 'He is not a troublemaker and his hair is only the same as those lads down in the Falklands.' (Daily Telegraph)

A sign in the lift of a large Tokyo department store says: 'NO PUSHING EXCEPT IN AN EMERGENCY.' (*Daily Telegraph*)

Followers of Maharishi Mahesh Yogi have announced a quick-response force of meditators has been formed, to rush to political hot spots the world over. According to Bevan Morris, President of Maharishi University in Washington, the 300-member élite force would be airlifted to a crisis area (he didn't say if they would use planes, or some other means), and would 'eliminate turbulence' by the radiation given off when they meditate together. (*Washington Post*)

Under a new traffic law in Peking, pedestrians can no longer cross the street where they wish. Now, they have to cross at special crosswalks, or pay an 18p fine. But an exception is made for people over 70, who are allowed to cross anywhere. As to whether that's doing senior citizens a favour – we'll have to wait until the fatality statistics start rolling in. (AP, San Francisco Examiner)

Peking police who raided a party at Huai-Chieh's pad, in response to neighbours' complaints, were taken aback by what they saw. According to the *Peking Daily*, the lights were low, the music 'unhealthy', the dance styles 'vulgar' and 'some people embraced . . . and acted contemptibly'. Twelve people were fined, fourteen received warnings, and seven others were locked up. (*San Francisco Chronicle*)

Dogs would have to wear diapers when away from home, under a bill before the Massachusetts legislature. The proposal, subject to approval by local communities, would subject owners of bare-bottomed pooches to fines of between $20 and $100. ('P.D.', *St Louis Post-Dispatch*)

Talk about sexual harassment on the job – staff at the satirical magazine Private Eye *have been getting more than their share, a London planning appeal hearing was told. According to George Beach, a representative for the magazine, the magazine's offices are regularly mistaken for a brothel. That has less to do with the behaviour of the staff than with the location of the offices – upstairs from a sex shop. Beach said that sex shop customers regularly climb the stairs and proposition secretaries. The hearing was dealing with an appeal of a ruling that would crack down on sex-related businesses in the Soho district.* (The Times)

Mayor C. Vernon Ayers of Kingston, Georgia, has finally found a celebrity to attend the town's historical festival – Wally Amos, the *Famous Amos* of chocolate chip cookie fame. The mayor had broadcast his desperate search for somebody famous far and wide, though he expressed a personal preference for Dolly Parton. But the town couldn't offer any money, and so it was 'no money, no celebrity' until Amos came along. Mayor Ayers says he's never heard of Amos but accepts the word of Amos's PR man that he is indeed a celebrity. (*St Louis Post-Dispatch*)

Every morning, Jim and Lillian Barbery have the blues; that's because their hen Goldie lays only blue eggs. The Cornwall pensioners say poultry experts have labelled Goldie a 'freak of nature'. (*Sunday Express*)

Police in the Netherlands village of Keerbeek were questioning a latter-day Noah about an estimated 250,000 stuffed animals and birds found in concrete bomb shelters in his back yard. 72-year-old John Roeleveld said God had told him to collect and mount two of every species in preparation for the end of the world, which is near. He said that after Judgement Day the creatures would rise rejuvenated. Police equipped with gas masks raided the shelter in response to neighbours' complaints. Roeleveld was not upset that his collection was being removed, saying: 'For each one they take I will get a hundred back. They will return to me of their own accord.' And that would make the neighbours even more upset. (San Francisco Chronicle)

Robins returning to Chicago have been turning to booze when they find their food supply cut off by frozen and snowy ground. The result is drunken robins who sometimes smash into cars. So reports Cook County Forest Preserve Naturalist Michael Conrath. He says the unavailability of food on the ground has turned the birds to last season's berries left on trees. The fermented berries have a high alcohol content. (UPI, *Los Angeles Times*)

Driving instructor Graham Butler, of Sherwood, Notts, thought he had prepared his student driver for every eventuality. But the driving manuals didn't mention the type of naked aggression displayed by one pedestrian. The man, who was wearing no clothes, came running down the middle of the road and took a flying leap on to the car's bonnet, landing with a crash and shattering the windscreen. Said Butler later: 'Luckily I told my pupil to stop; otherwise it would have been much worse.' The leaper was hospitalised with minor injuries. Police were investigating. (*Daily Telegraph*)

Can a foreigner with a strange accent, life-style and religion receive a friendly reception when he decides to live in rural Georgia? Oh yes, the folks in Kingston, Georgia, population 731, are switching on that celebrated southern hospitality for the newcomer, Saudi Arabian Prince Faisal Mohammed Saud Al-Kabir. He has purchased 3,500 prime acres adjoining Kingston, and plans to build a palace and do a little landscaping – polo grounds, seven lakes, that kind of thing. 'This could be the key to our future,' says Mayor Vernon Ayers, 'I'll bet he could underwrite the entire $1.3 million it would take to build a sewer system. I even kidded him that we ought to expand the city limits to include his property. And you know what, he didn't laugh.' (Atlanta Constitution/Journal)

When Red Cross nurses conducted a blood drive at the Elysium Institute in Topanga, outside Los Angeles, not many people rolled up sleeves, but it was a success anyway. Elysium is a nudist colony. (*Los Angeles Times*)

When Archie Arnold realised his time was up, he had a last request to make. As a result, two parking meters now stand over his grave at a Fort Wayne, Indiana, cemetery. Says his lawyer: 'You had to know Archie.' The meters, of course, say 'expired'. (*Jet Magazine*)

Charles Berlitz could speak four languages fluently before he could read, and since then he's added another twelve languages, plus another fifteen where he says he 'gets along'. That's an achievement befitting the grandson of the founder of the Berlitz Language Schools, and makes him well qualified to write his latest book, *Native Tongues*, which is a collection of little-known facts and anecdotes about languages. For instance, did you know that German just missed out being chosen the official

27

language of the United States, losing to English by one vote at the continental congress in Philadelphia? Did you know that Chicago, literally translated, means 'The Place of the Skunk Cabbage', while Manhattan means 'The Place of the Great Drunkenness'? Or that in Japan, you compliment a woman on her beauty by comparing her face to 'an egg with eyes'? Berlitz has found that, though the exact language changes from culture to culture, proverbs remain pretty similar in meaning. For instance, 'Don't count your chickens before they're hatched' becomes, in German, 'You can't hang people before you've caught them'. (*Chicago Tribune*)

Some parents give their kids sports equipment as gifts. Los Angeles sports tycoon Jerry Buss gives his kids entire franchises. Buss, who owns the LA Lakers and Kings, last year bought his 20-year-old daughter Jeannie a professional tennis team, the LA Strings. And last month he bought his son John, 25, a pro indoor soccer team, to be called the LA Lazers. Son Jim, 23, isn't into team sports so much, but dad has given him authority to buy thoroughbred race-horses. Says John: 'In a way, this is really like a toy. But it's an educational toy, like ... building blocks or an erector set.' 20-year-old Jeannie, who has her own 24-room wing at Daddy's Pacific Palisades Mansion, says: 'Some people get the wrong impression of me. I mean, I went to a State school. I didn't get a car (that's her BMW) until I was 17, not 16 like most kids.' (Los Angeles Times)

The unemployment situation drove Timothy Roy right up a tree, and he intends to stay there for a year, atop a 20-foot tree in Norwalk, California, in a treehouse. Actually, the tree is made of fibreglass and steel, but that's good enough for the *Guinness Book of Records* people. Roy, a 29-year-old unemployed actor, hopes his going out on a limb will land him a role in a comedy or horror movie when he descends next year. His treehouse is stocked with a TV, video equipment, a toilet, and he hopes soon to have a shower and phone. A basket hoisted by a rope will deliver his food, which he says will be donated by local restaurants, and his fan mail. (*Los Angeles Herald-Examiner*)

Sy Freedman of Silver Spring, Maryland, received a collection notice from the Washington Hospital Centre threatening to turn his unpaid account over to an attorney or collection agency. The sum owing? One cent. (*Washington Post*)

Washington Post *night editor Joe Bouchard reports that a kid phoned the paper at 4 am on the night of the lunar eclipse to report that Pac Man had swallowed the moon.* (Washington Post)

The University of Wisconsin has come up with a form letter for all the people who've contacted the school about a man who identifies himself as an Economics Professor there. The man approaches people at airports, mostly older women, and asks for a short-term loan, saying he's run a bit short. The University's form letter says: 'I am very, very sorry to inform you that there is no Paul Phillips.' (*Los Angeles Times*)

According to the results of a gallup poll conducted in Japan, only 22 per cent of Japanese men surveyed said they would fight for their country in the event of war. Now, if it were a matter of fighting for their corporation . . . (*The Guardian*)

A Manhattan lawyer was delighted to get his stolen BMW back, the New York Times *reports, particularly since, in the twelve days it was missing, it had undergone several thousand dollars worth of improvements, including expensive racing seats, wire wheels, a fancy steering wheel, fog lights and a much better radio. In some ways, the lawyer had to regret that the car was recovered so quickly. He said: 'Another week and I might have had a sun roof.'* (New York Times)

Man-eating piranhas, those charming fish, schools of which have the God-given ability to strip a man to the bone in seconds, have turned up in the Ohio and Missouri rivers, says biologist Robert McCauley, of Wilfrid Laurier University in Waterloo, Ontario, Canada. They got there, he says, because 'People buy these things as pets, and when they get bored they let them loose in the rivers or flush them down their toilets.' (*Toronto Globe*)

Tourists in Zimbabwe's Mana Pools National Park began offering elephants oranges to get close-up photos of them. Now, park wardens are warning, the elephants have become so addicted to oranges that they'll trample anything that stands between them and an orange, in their rush to grab the fruit. (Reuters, *Washington Post*)

According to Barbara Robinson, a service representative with the San Diego Gas and Electric Co., a man phoned requesting that service be discontinued, and just then a blackout hit his district. He shouted, 'Not now!' (Los Angeles Daily News)

Some Boston motorists have been beating that city's parking meters by spray-painting them so they can't be read. Officials say over 400 meters have been tampered with in this manner. (*Los Angeles Daily News*)

The most widely subscribed-to magazine among inmates at Britain's Nottingham Prison is not some skin magazine, according to authorities. It's something that is even more exciting – *Country Homes*, a glossy magazine that deals with the stately mansions of the rich, as well as titbits about the doings of the leisure class and the price of Ritzy silverware. Says a prison spokesman: 'A lot of it is fantasy. They sit there and dream of what they are going to do when they get out and plan their movements.' (*The Guardian*)

Unreasonably dangerous meal

A Pittsburgh couple who allegedly suffered thumb cuts that became infected, while peeling rock shrimp, have filed a $10,000 lawsuit against an Annapolis, Maryland, seafood restaurant. Neil and Susan Cohen charge that the restaurant served them an 'unreasonably dangerous' meal. (*Miami Herald*)

Johan and Barbara Krarup claim that when they moved into their bungalow in Grosmont, Gwent, South Wales, three years ago, they had no idea that a public footpath ran through their property. But now they've been informed by the Gwent County Council that not only does a footpath run across their property, it runs right through their sun lounge and possibly their kitchen as well. The Council added in a letter that, unless they reopen the path, they could face legal action. Says Mr Krarup, 'The whole thing's ludicrous. Nobody's used the path for over thirty years.' An elderly neighbour, Trevor Davies, recalls that the footpath goes back to the days when people had to haul water from a well and a gentleman's agreement allowed them to cross different fields. A spokesman for the County Council says that it has a legal obligation to ensure that recognised footpaths stay open. Well, maybe the Krarups can persuade strollers to at least wipe their feet before walking through. (*Sunday Express*)

The Pretoria Supreme Court in South Africa has upheld the appeal of a woman convicted of living in an area of Johannesburg reserved for whites. Cynthia Freeman was convicted in Johannesburg of violating the 'Group Areas Act', despite her contention that she is white. The judge ruled that she had failed to prove she was 'obviously white', although she has blonde hair, blue eyes and pale skin. Her conviction followed several days of intense courtroom debate over the height of her cheekbones and the flatness of her nose. Miss Freeman contended that her nose had been flattened in a car accident. The High Court has now supported her. (The Times)

The US Supreme Court has refused to hear the appeal of a Seattle man who sued the Washington State Bar Association, claiming the group is hindering his efforts to spread the news about his amazing discovery. George McLean Campbell says he has discovered that air may be 'an intelligent form of life . . . that blows and moves by means of its own life and will'. A Federal Judge decided Campbell's suit was hot air, and he has an appeal pending before a US Circuit Court. But he had asked the Supreme Court to step in because of his discovery's great importance to the 'national welfare'. The Supreme Court justices did not comment on why they refused to hear the case. (*Vancouver Sun*)

A man who killed a Pontiac, Michigan, couple in a head-on collision that occurred when he drove his car down the wrong side of the highway filed suit for damages against their estate. 28-year-old Andrew Collier claimed that the victims, Sigmund and Irene Fitz, were partially at fault because they could have swerved out of the way. Collier told an Oakland County Court jury in Pontiac that, due in part to the negligence of the victims, his life is now a mess. He walks with a limp, suffers slurred speech, and one leg and arm are virtually useless. He said he is unable to work. Judge George La Platta ruled that the results of a blood test that showed Collier had been drinking could not be introduced because the test was improperly administered. After two hours of deliberation, the jury decided his case had no merit. (*San Francisco Chronicle*)

For lawyers, this could turn out to be bigger than plane crashes, if a lawsuit filed by 24-year-old Susan Liptrot of Fort Lauderdale, Florida has a favourable outcome. She wants $100,000 from the unidentified Fort Lauderdale man who gave her herpes after, she maintains, he had deceived her into thinking he was herpes-free. And it wasn't that he was wearing one of those ambiguous buttons that say 'herpes free'. It was in the cold light of the next morning that Liptrot says she discovered a tell-tale sore on the defendant's body. By then it was too late. (San Francisco Chronicle)

An allegation in a $500,000 lawsuit, that charged a high school with negligence for selling huge oatmeal cakes, because of their danger when used in food fights, has been dismissed by a judge in Oxnard, California. 16-year-old John Taylor lost the vision in his left eye when he was struck by a large oatmeal projectile during one of the frequent food fights at the Oxnard Union High School. His lawsuit claimed that 'large, circular cookies were regularly used for the purpose of assaulting and battering others by throwing them in a manner similar to a discuss or frisbee, thereby imparting great velocity, force and destructive capability to said cookie'. However, the negligence claim crumbled in the court of Superior Court Judge William Peck, who agreed with school officials that they couldn't be expected to restrain cookie sales because of the cookies' 'aerodynamic qualities'. However, the judge did let stand another allegation that school officials did not adequately supervise the quadrangle where such food fights took place. (*Sacramento Bee*)

Admittedly the party at their Fountain, Colorado home was loud, even after midnight, but party hosts John Snow and Fred Wilson feel that authorities overreacted when they sent a military strike force, armed with M-16s, to break it up. Neighbours were more upset about the late-night military invasion of their neighbourhood than they were about the party. Now Snow and Wilson, along with two neighbours, have filed an $800,000 lawsuit against the US Government, high-ranking officers at Fort Carson, where the strategic force was based, and 1st Lt Kelly Siple, who led the troops into action. Army officials apparently acted after being informed that several dozen soldiers were at the party. The soldiers were transported back to base. (*Denver Post*)

Three men who tried to paddle a bathtub 150 miles around the east coast of England, in order to raise £500 for medical research, had to be plucked from their tub by the coastguard, at a cost many times that amount. The three – Anthony Proctor, John Nichol and Martin Bastin-Northcott – all of Peterborough, were drifting helplessly out into the North Sea when they were rescued. Commander Michael Grubb, a coastguard spokesman at the Great Yarmouth station, said the men had ignored instructions to have a radio with them, and a cabin cruiser alongside. (Daily Telegraph)

Police were ready to hear a sad song after they received a call from 34-year-old Johnnie Brown Jr, in Madison, Wisconsin, saying that he had just broken into the Good Shepherd Lutheran Church, but was now ready to atone for his sins. They could come and get him at the church, he said. He'd be playing the piano while he waited. (*Washington Post*)

A gesture by the Pope, when he arrived in England on his visit, has set off a new craze among passengers arriving at London's Gatwick Airport – kissing the tarmac as he did. Says an airport spokesman: 'The idea has certainly caught on. One passenger does it and the whole planeload follows suit. I suppose we will have to look at double-cleaning the tarmac if this craze goes on much longer.' (*Daily Telegraph*)

A member of the City Council in Wolverhampton, England took some shocking action to deal with children who were chasing their balls into his vegetable garden. He electrified his fence. Archibald Findlay placed a 115-volt wire on his 6-foot fence. That was a jolt to several children, and to their mothers, who complained to police. They took the fence down. (Daily Express)

San Diego police sergeant Jack Docherty had the rare distinction of arresting two drunk drivers in one car – a man working the pedals, and a woman, seated on his lap, who was doing the steering. It was a double bust in more than one way. The woman was also charged with public nudity. (*San Diego Union*)

An Appeal Court has overturned the drunken driving conviction of Kenneth Collins of Crawley, Sussex, despite evidence that his urine sample showed twice the legal limit of alcohol. The Court acted after hearing that Collins' urine sample also showed the presence of micro-organisms capable of producing alcohol on their own. Thus, it wasn't clear whether he had drunk too much, or whether the little bugs inside him had just produced too much. (*The Times*)

36

A new system introduced by Britain's Department of Health and Social Security which has patients writing their own sick-excuse notes for short absences from work, instead of taking up their doctors' time with note requests, has produced some real howlers, says the Department. The notes have uncovered some conditions previously unknown to medical science. One man's excuse was a 'fluid stomach'. A Somerset man said he was 'mentally unstable', and was 'staying in bed until a psychiatrist comes'. A farmer reported suffering 'grazing on the knee' and a Gloucester woman said she was 'sick and tired due to the doctor's tablets'. Another woman reported she was suffering from 'desperation', and another man said his problem was 'bleeding noise'. (*Daily Telegraph*)

A sort of hotel guide for Rock 'n' Roll musicians is nearing completion, written by veteran drummer Carmine Appice. It's called 'The International Guide to Hotel Wrecking'. (Los Angeles Times)

After fifteen years of trying to pass his driving test, 32-year-old Michael Webber of Ivybridge, England finally succeeded on his thirtieth attempt. Having passed this milestone, he now intends to go after a lorry driver's licence. (*Daily Telegraph*)

Psychology Today reports that a California firm marketing $25 psychological test kits, which the test subject completes and then sends back for a computer analysis, has benefited from an unexpected marketing bonanza. Some people are buying the psychological tests as gifts for friends and relatives. It certainly must be nice for the recipient of such a gift to know that people care. (*Psychology Today*)

Communist activist Angela Davis won't be getting the key to the city of Miami, which so many other people have recently received from Miami commissioner Joe Carollo, in his role as deputy mayor. A strong representation on behalf of Ms Davis was made by a man who walked into Carollo's office, and demanded that she receive this honour, or else he'd blow up the world. An assistant phoned the police, and the man was taken to a Crisis Intervention Centre. (Miami Herald)

A two-day rampage by thousands of rioters in the small southern Italian town of Nocera Inferiore left hundreds of thousands of pounds worth of damage. Fifteen buses were set on fire, roads and railway lines leading out of town were blocked, passing cars were damaged, and schools were forced to close when mobs stormed them. The rioting was triggered by an Italian Soccer Federation decision to promote another team, instead of the Nocera team, up to the league's second division. (*Daily Telegraph*)

Thirty-year-old Ray Reed's alleged crime left him with no way out, that he could find. He broke into a Rye, New York house, but then couldn't locate the exit, and had to awaken a sleeping resident for directions on how to get out. The resident complied, but gave police a good description of the lost soul, which led to his arrest. (*Sacramento Bee*)

What some rock fans will go through to hear a favourite band! According to Record World *magazine, two fans were nailed trying to catch a recent sold-out* Black Sabbath *concert at the New Haven (Conn.) Coliseum by drilling a hole through the ceiling.* (Record World)

The Soviet newspaper *Trud* has some good news and bad news for the many Russian housewives who like to make their own jam and other preserves. The good news is that production of the jars used for preserving has kept pace with the demand for them. The bad news is that they forgot to make lids for the jars. A severe shortage of lids is now being forecast, and the long-suffering Russian housewife has been left in a jam, or a pickle. (*The Times*)

A 23-year-old woman who urinated into a policeman's hat was relieved all the more when a judge in Vancouver, Canada, decided that the mischief charge against her didn't hold any water. Provincial Court Judge Keith Libby cited the doctrine of 'necessity' in dismissing the charge, in that the woman had to go, and the hat was the only receptacle around in the room in the police station where she was being held. The woman had been picked up for investigation of a theft. Just before she was released without charges, she asked for permission to use the washroom, and said that a police officer told her to shut up. She couldn't shut up. Well, police constable Dave Anderson had left his hat in the room, and nature's call was becoming stronger. The prosecutor asked the woman: 'Did you try to put the hat back where you found it?' She replied: 'Yes, I do have manners.' Anderson has since been issued with a new hat. (*Vancouver Sun*)

The State of Nevada has been looking for a State symbol. Among proposed symbols being considered are a blackjack hand, a slot machine and, to commemorate the biggest gamble of them all, an atom bomb going off – in honour of the State's role as a host to nuclear tests. (St Louis Post-Dispatch)

In his twelve years of golfing, says 66-year-old Howard Hewitt, 'I had my dreams of something special happening to me on a golf course – but I never expected them to come three at a time.' The retired civil servant from

Everton, Liverpool, got a hole-in-one on his favourite golf course. Then, the next day, he holed-in-one on a nearby course. As he and his golfing partners stood on the green trying to calculate the odds against two holes-in-one on consecutive days, a wayward golf ball from an adjoining fairway hit him on the back of the head and knocked him out cold. (*Sunday Express*)

Tucson resident Byron Ivancovich has filed a suit against city officials, alleging that he suffers emotional damage every time he drives past a statue of the Mexican bandito Pancho Villa, which the city has installed in a park alongside a major thoroughfare. The life-size statue is a gift to the city from Mexico, where Villa is considered a revolutionary hero. Ivancovich's attorney, Michael J. Rusing, says he heard some stomach-turning stories when he interviewed survivors of Villa's 1916 raid on a New Mexican border town, during which sixteen residents were killed. Rusing says the statue glorifies 'a murderer and rapist, thus corrupting public morals, driving customers from downtown Tucson, and creating an eyesore'. (*Washington Post*)

The May Co. department store chain has filed a $2 million lawsuit against the owners of two small planes that collided in mid-air over the Los Angeles suburb of Sherman Oaks. One of the planes crashed into a May Co. store, killing the pilot, and, says the suit, 'substantially interfering with the plaintiff's business operations'. The US Govt. was also named. (Los Angeles Herald-Examiner)

When State District Judge Bruce Wettman, in Houston, found no jurors on hand for a divorce case, he sent out for twelve men from the 'Star of Hope' mission, feeling they'd appreciate the chance to pick up a few bucks. The jurors took their duties seriously, awarding the woman

$8,000, and Judge Wettman was impressed by the way they rose to the occasion, by 'combing their hair and tucking in their shirts'. (*San Diego Union*)

The lobbying by builder Abraham Hirschfeld and two associates was too intense for Dorothy Green, who was Director of New York City's Office of Environmental Impact at the time. The millionaire Brooklyn builder was seeking a permit when he and his cohorts visited Green in her office, locked the door, and wouldn't allow her to use the phone for an hour. As a result of their pressure, a Mineola, New York Court was told, Green has been unable to work or have good sex ever since. The 54-year-old Freeport, NY woman was suing for $16 million. The Court awarded her an undisclosed sum. (*Washington Post*)

A British job-recruiting firm that told a scientist from New Zealand that it wouldn't recommend him for a job because New Zealanders are 'nomads' has been found guilty of racial discrimination in violation of Britain's Race Relations Act. An industrial tribunal at Newcastle-upon-Tyne ordered the firm Hoggett Bower Search to pay Dr Peter Melling £500 for 'hurt feelings'. (The Times)

Jewellery store owner John McLaughlin has filed a $7,500 lawsuit against the city of Grants Pass, Oregon, because Grants Pass police failed to catch a youth who broke into his store and made off with $9,700 worth of goods. McLaughlin says police were negligent – they should have checked the fire escape, which here appears to have served as the burglar escape. A teenager later admitted to the theft, but none of the stolen property was recovered. (*Portland Oregonian*)

Rock bands have cut back on their touring, complaining about the expenses involved. But present expenses will be chicken feed compared to potential costs if Michael Valdenerso's lawsuit is successful. Valdenerso is suing the owners of Duffy's Tavern in Eugene, Oregon, and the Hot Whacks Band, for $405,000 over a 50 to 60 per cent hearing loss he says he suffered listening to the band one night in 1980. (*Los Angeles Daily News*)

The snails that San Diego's 'Limehouse' restaurant served to Nancy Tattoli were fresh. One snail got a bit too fresh and tried to climb off the dinner plate. That, Tattoli says, in a lawsuit filed in San Diego Superior Court, made her 'disgusted and distressed'. In her attempt to get away, she fell down the stairs. She wants $350,000 for emotional and physical damages. (Los Angeles Daily News)

Thieves did a thorough job of cleaning out Gordon and Ann Downie's home in Fife, Scotland. The Downies and their four children had temporarily moved to another home. Downie returned to find not only the house gone, but also the garage, the barn, the greenhouse, the garden shed, the fence and even the plants. (*The Guardian*)

A man in the Canadian town of Sydney, Nova Scotia, who sued his former fiancée for the return of $3,492 in gifts and money he had given her during their ten-year courtship, plus interest on them, has had his breach of contract claim rejected. County Court Judge Allan Sullivan ruled that Patrick Nardocchio's gifts were simply Christmas or birthday presents, and not intended for their joint use after marriage. The woman did return her engagement and wedding rings. Judge Sullivan said that Nardocchio's legal action was probably triggered when he saw her with another man after their split. (*Toronto Globe & Mail*)

Charles Waites had special reasons for being upset at the Jehovah's Witness evangelist who came knocking at the door of his home. The Blue Springs, Missouri police officer wasn't in, but his wife Karon Ann listened intently as the missionary told her that her husband was an 'agent of the devil'. Jehovah's Witnesses believe that all governments are run by Satan. Shortly thereafter, Karon Ann left Charles. Now a judge in Jackson County, Missouri, has awarded him $75,000 in an 'alienation of affections' suit against the evangelist, Judy Marshall. (Intro Magazine)

A robot has popped up in the most unlikely of places – as a tour guide at a stately thirteenth-century mansion near Lancaster. Stanley Crabtree, owner of the Elizabethan residence, Thurnham Hall, says that the 6-foot tall robot, who dresses as an Elizabethan knight, is 'more efficient' than the two human guides he replaced. Says Crabtree: 'We used to find children got restless listening to the previous guides. With this fellow, they listen to every word and stay attentive.' (*Daily Telegraph*)

The Florida Supreme Court has reprimanded Circuit Judge W. Fred Turner of Panama City for his arrogance and abuse of powers. Among complaints cited against the judge was his jailing of two witnesses who offered contradictory testimony, on the grounds that one of them was lying, and a visit he paid to a woman who had prevailed in a child custody case before him. He dropped in on her trailer home, armed with a probing flashlight, three times in one night, to check if any man was spending the night there. He'll continue to serve on the bench. (*Miami Herald*)

Some might accuse Ann Challa of not making her money honestly, but she's laughing all the way to the bank. When it comes to laughing, Challa is a real pro. The

Hollywood woman charges comedians $100 and upwards to sit in the audience and crack up at their jokes. Her professional laughter is infectious enough to ignite an audience. And she has the stamina. Challa holds the world record, in fact, for the longest laugh – 4 hours and 6 minutes. She's also a serious actress, but says it's the laughing she enjoys most. 'Believe me,' she says, 'I can laugh at anything.' (New Woman)

Bill Blair is one of the few business people who takes pride in how lousy his product is. Blair, owner of V.C.I. Co. in Tulsa, is offering a line of video cassettes of old movies, about which he says: 'These films had bad photography, bad staging and bad acting.' In fact, he says, 'They're some of the worst movies ever made.' And that's the point. For instance, 'They Saved Hitler's Brain' has to be seen to be believed. (*Entrepreneur* magazine)

Researcher Dr Michel Dugust-Rouilee of Nantes, France, reports that he checked out French families having titles of nobility, like 'Count' and 'Marquis' and found that 20,000 of 25,000 families checked were phonies. (*The Times*)

The Colorado Court of Appeals has unanimously rejected a woman's claim that she shouldn't have to pay $46,000 in damages to the sleeping occupants of a house into which her car crashed because, she maintained, the sleeping occupants should be considered 'pedestrians'. They would then come under Colorado's No-Fault Auto Insurance Law. Peggy Margaret Simpson had crashed through a wall and into a child's bedroom after her car went out of control while she was returning from a party. She was successfully sued in Adams County District Court by Darvin and Jackie Smith and their two children. The court didn't agree that people asleep in their beds should be considered pedestrians. Now, if they had been sleepwalking, perhaps it would have been different. (*Los Angeles Daily News*)

Nobody makes a punch bag out of Sugar Ray Robinson, not without his permission. The former boxing champ has filed a $10 million lawsuit against Sport Fun Inc. for putting his face on a punch bag without authorisation from him. (Los Angeles Daily News)

Arlene Zuckerman of Valley Stream, New York, found the experience of biting into a beetle in her Dannon raspberry yoghurt so hair raising that, she says, her hair fell out. Her attorney, Abraham Fuchsberg, of Manhattan, told a Nassau County Jury in Mineola, NY: 'She is an unmarried young lady who looks like an Indian has scalped her.' The jury awarded her $425,000 in damages. Fuchsberg said his client was eating the yoghurt while watching TV, when she 'felt a piece of foreign matter in her mouth . . . she knew it was too hard to be a raspberry, and besides, it was moving . . . it is very sad what this girl has been through'. A member of her family managed to save the bug as evidence. (*San Francisco Chronicle*)

Actor Dustin Hoffman feels that when you are paying $7,000 a month in rent for an apartment, you should at least be able to get some heat out of the radiators and a regular flow of hot water. Absence of these amenities in his New York apartment has prompted Hoffman to sue the person he's subletting it from, Paul Brine, and the brokers involved. (*San Francisco Chronicle*)

A Colorado Springs, Colorado man who says some bad beer he drank caused him to develop a fear of beer, thus ruining his drinking life, has filed a $50,000 lawsuit. Named in Francis Kane's suit are the Olympia Brewing

Co. *and the liquor store that sold him the beer which made him sick. Said Kane: 'I used to enjoy beer. Now I'm afraid to drink it.'* (Los Angeles Daily News)

In Nashville, William T. Hardison is suing Elizabeth Ann Honig for $500 because she put a curse on his sex life. Hardison says that he and Honig used to be lovers in an 'up-and-down relationship', but it's pretty down right now. He says in his suit that he came bounding out of his house on a recent morning to take his 'beloved dog Fidel Castro for his morning constitutional', and beheld on his porch a dead chicken, a voodoo doll, and a note saying: 'A curse upon you, a curse upon your dog Fidel Castro. A curse upon your emotional and sexual relationships with every woman you are presently involved with or will ever be.' Hardison didn't explain why he only wants $500. (*Sacramento Bee*)

They may not know 'who put the bomp in the bomp she bomp she bomp', but three surviving members of the singing group 'The Rivingtons' know who took the 'Papa oom mow mow' from their song 'Papa Oom Mow Mow', and they're suing over it. The three – Alfred Frazier, Turner Wilson and John E. Harris – all of Los Angeles, have filed a $10 million lawsuit in the US District Court in LA against composer Dallas Frazier, MCA records and several other firms over the 1981 hit song by the Oak Ridge Boys, 'Elvira', which was written by Frazier, and which, they charge, contains their own 'Papa Oom Mow Mow' in a slightly different order. In the 1960s, the Rivingtons settled out of court with The Trashmen over a Trashmen hit that combined words from 'Papa Oom Mow Mow' with another Rivingtons classic – 'Bird-Bird-Bird-Bird-Bird's The Word'. (*San Francisco Chronicle*)

A 58-year-old Brooklyn man is suing Olympic Airways of Greece for $150,000 over some spilled coffee. Max Binder claims he became impotent after a stewardess spilled coffee on his lap when the plane hit rough air. The airline, citing a medical examiner's report made at Athens Airport, says that Binder has blown the extent of his injury way out of proportion. (Daily Telegraph)

More than 75 per cent of bald-headed or balding persons surveyed by *New Generation*, a Sparks, Nevada hair-products company, felt that they had been 'discriminated against both socially and in business' because of their lack of hair. Nearly 85 per cent of baldies (let's call them 'the hair-deprived') felt hair loss could lead to psychological problems. And 72 per cent felt that hairy-headed people were inconsiderate to the hair-deprived. (*Los Angeles Times*)

County Councillors in Worcestershire are satisfied with the present name of their council district – Inkberrow, and they're fighting to keep it. They've described as 'ridiculous and absurd' the suggestion by a Boundaries Commission of a new name for their district – Flyford Piddle. (*Daily Telegraph*)

A brush with death turned into a hair-raising experience for Nashville funeral director Joe Baltz. The 63-year-old mortician almost died of a heart ailment, but a drug administered to revive him, spironolactone, also revived his scalp, which had been dormant and completely bald for fifteen years. He now has a full shock of white hair. The drug inhibits the production of the male hormone testosterone, which is implicated in baldness, according to Baltz's doctor, Michael Miller. (*Orlando Sentinel*)

The kangaroo was named by explorer Captain Cook. He asked an Australian native what the name of that strange jumping animal was. The native replied: 'Kangaroo.' Only much later was it learned that 'kangaroo' in the local dialect means 'what did you say?' (Daily Mail)

Lakeview, New York police officers Leonard Sawyer and William Portz feared the worst when they came across a man slumped over his car's steering wheel, with a boa constrictor wrapped around his neck. But, as it turned out, 26-year-old John Caputo, of Elmont, New York was only dozing, and 'Chadwick', his pet boa, was himself relaxing, in his comfortable perch around Caputo's neck. Caputo was taken in on a charge of drunken driving, and Chadwick had to find another neck. He was turned over to Caputo's relatives. (*Los Angeles Times*)

Pest control experts in Norwich were marvelling at a family of mice which they discovered thriving in a meat freezer, at temperatures of -15 degrees Farenheit. They lived on frozen meat carcasses, and survived the deep freeze conditions by growing thick woolly fur coats. 'They were just like little balls of fluff,' said Norwich Chief Public Health Officer Tony Welch. Just how hardy the mice had become was discovered by Ministry of Agriculture scientists who fed them rat poison. They thrived on it. (*Daily Telegraph*)

An FBI agent who infiltrated into the high echelons of an alleged Mafia family during 6½ years of undercover work will have to reveal his identity at an upcoming murder conspiracy trial, despite the reports of informants that the mob will kill him if he is identified. Defendant Benjamin Ruggiero, for one, is quoted as saying that he would kill the agent if it was the last thing he did. However, US District Court Judge Robert W. Sweet ruled in New York that the agent will have to be named, despite the danger, to avoid prejudicing the jury. Judge Sweet said that if the agent were to testify anonymously, the jurors might get the impression that the agent had received death threats, and that wouldn't be fair. (Washington Post)

James McRea, of Lyons, Nebraska, who lost his driver's licence in Iowa a few months ago for failing to provide a urine sample that would show if he was drunk, has had the licence restored by a judge in Sioux City who was satisfied that he was dry. Lyons said he tried to provide the requested sample, but couldn't, since he had just let it all out shortly before he was stopped. The Iowa Department of Transportation had ruled that this was no excuse, but Woodbury County District Court Judge Charles Woole decided that, if McRae held no water, his defence did hold water. (*San Francisco Chronicle*)

Does a prison inmate have the right to a daily marijuana ration, if he smokes it for religious purposes? A court may have to decide, since authorities at the federally run Metropolitan Corrections Centre, in the Miami area, aren't too keen on granting Thomas Reilly Jr's request. Reilly, otherwise known as 'Brother Louv', is spiritual leader of the local Ethiopian Zion Coptic Church. He's serving ten years for pot smuggling. Brother Louv says that smoking pot for sacramental purposes is a 'centuries old' tradition of Copts worldwide, and that he has the right to marijuana in prison, just as communal wine is allowed in. (*Miami Herald*)

A Chinese appliance factory has developed what it calls 'the electric cat', the Workers' Daily *reports. The device zaps mice with a lethal charge of electricity, and then goes 'meow, meow'.* (Los Angeles Daily News)

At the weddings that Barry Summers performs, the bride and groom prefer that, instead of rice, the guests throw bones. Summers, who lives in the Chicago suburb of Orland Park, performs weddings for dogs, cats and other species, although he had his doubts when a man asked him to marry a macaw and a boa constrictor. He never heard from the man after their phone conversation – perhaps the pair were united before they could get legally hitched. And it is a legal wedding that Summers performs, with a legal wedding certificate, since he is a legally ordained minister. He charges a basic $50 to tie the leash. That includes flowers and a three-tier wedding cake moulded from hamburger or pet food. For extra money, he'll supply the wedding outfits, which might include a veil, a silk-flowered white leash and collar and lace anklets for the bride, and a top hat, bow tie and ankle ribbons for the groom. Grooms supply their own tails. (*Vancouver Sun*)

This one's bound to raise a few hairs: Russian car buyers generally have to wait up to two years to take delivery of a new car they've ordered. But a Soviet fur plant has been advertising a special deal – immediate delivery of a new Zhigali car to anyone handing in 1,000 dog pelts and 500 cat skins. One newspaper is speculating that this may be behind an increase in reports of missing pets. (*The Times*)

Psychologists at the University of California at Davis hung around the check-out counters at twenty-eight different supermarkets, and found that half the customers told employees to 'have a nice day'. (Intro magazine)

In Baker, Oregon, 48-year-old Roger Glynn Payton bet a fellow bar patron a beer that he could lie on a street until four cars drove by. He lost when his luck ran flat under car number three. No word on whether the winner will try to collect the beer from Payton's estate. (*San Diego Union*)

Frank Crookston of West Covina, California says that he was stranded for two hours trying to thumb a ride until he wrote out a sign that said 'Home to Mother'; seven minutes later, he was picked up. (*Los Angeles Times*)

Three prisoners managed to escape from the Southern Michigan Prison in Jackson by hailing a taxi. They were wearing civilian clothes, and managed to blend in with a minimum security maintenance crew working outside the walls. They found a waiting cab in the car park. (Sacramento Bee)

Pickle Packers International of Chicago wants Americans to remember that America was named after a one-time pickle salesman, Amerigo Vespucci. The Italian-born adventurer–explorer began his maritime career by selling provisions, including kegs of pickles, to ocean-going vessels. Finally he decided to venture out into the brine himself. (*Sacramento Bee*)

In Carson City, Nevada, book-keeper Sharon Walling thought her parking ticket was a load of ... well, she expressed her sentiments when she paid $10 bail, pending a court fight, with a check written on a toilet plunger. The plunger was cashed at a local bank. (*Palm Springs Desert Sun*)

When he's not drinking or taking drugs he's the greatest person around

IRAN has announced some economising measures in its fight against drug smuggling, but that doesn't mean that convicted smugglers can breathe easier. The head of Iran's drug courts, Ayatollah Ahmed Zarger, has announced that drug smugglers will now be hanged instead of being executed by firing squads, in order to save on the cost of bullets. (from the *Economist*, in 'Inquiry')

The democratic tide was strong enough to carry a dead man into office in a Texas district that stretches from the edge of Austin to the Gulf Coast. State Senator John Wilson, who died on 19 September, was re-elected with more than 66 per cent of the vote, compared to 32 per cent for his Republican opponent. Democrats tried to replace him on the ballot, but were told by Secretary of State David Dean, a Republican, that it was too late. The results prove that it's never too late. (*San Francisco Chronicle*)

Harold 'Brookie' Broome from Texas was simply overwhelmed by the recognition he received at a Chamber of Commerce banquet honouring him as San Angelo's Citizen of the Year. The 53-year-old Broome accepted his award, made some remarks and, finishing up, collapsed and died. (San Francisco Examiner)

The US Internal Revenue Service has accused a Colorado couple of posing as CIA agents on a secret assignment in order to obtain free breast-enlargement surgery for the woman. William R. and Patricia Anne Golightly allegedly told a cosmetic surgeon that larger breasts were essential for their mission. The surgeon was paid with a $2,500 personal cheque, and was told that the government would soon deposit the funds to cover it. As it turned out, the cheque had more bounce than Mrs Golightly's brand new breasts. (*Washington Post*)

Even though she was burned in love, Ladonna May Martin's passions still flamed for her old torch. She begged a judge in Flagstaff, Arizona, not to send her boyfriend to jail for drenching her in gasoline and setting her on fire four months ago..Showing no visible signs of the burns, she told Coconino County Superior Court Judge John H. Grace: 'We love each other and I don't want Larry to go to prison. When he's not drinking or taking drugs, he's the greatest person in the world.' But the unmoved judge threw cold water on their red-hot love and sentenced 27-year-old Larry Eagans to seven years. (*Los Angeles Times*)

The family of a deceased Philippino man is suing a Manila funeral parlour for shortening his legs to fit him in a coffin. The family had paid $2,000 for a special coffin to accommodate the man who was 6 feet 5 inches tall before the alterations were performed. (*Reuters*, Los Angeles Times)

Milorad Jovanovic received a new lease of life in Vienna's Wilhelmina Hospital, when surgeons installed a pacemaker in his chest, but he hadn't required a new lease – his old one was still good. The 50-year-old Yugoslav cemetery worker had checked into the hospital for treatment for rheumatism pains, then broke a leg in a hospital fall. He got the pacemaker due to a language misunderstanding. Doctors agreed to take it back. (*Los Angeles Times*)

Britain's *Gateshead Post* reported that a mother had complained that her son had been injured by new toughened glass windows that had replaced windows broken by vandals at a local clinic. The mother said her son suffered a head injury when a rock he hurled at the strengthened glass bounced back and hit him in the head. (*Punch*)

Black motorists in the Los Angeles suburb of Pacoima have been given some very important driving safety tips concerning what to do when stopped by the police. Jose de Sosa, President of the San Fernando Branch of the NAACP, told blacks gathered at a special seminar: 'Keep your hands on the steering wheel. Do not make any sudden, jerky moves. If you are asked for a driver's licence, before you reach, tell the policeman where it is located, for instance, say: "I'm going to get my wallet. I'm using my right hand." These are ways lives can be saved.' (Los Angeles Times)

State officials were investigating the complaint of a Sun City, Florida widow that she was burnt by a Largo, Florida crematorium. 50-year-old Ursula H. Smith said that the ashes she received back from the National Cremation Society were not those of her husband. She could tell because the ashes contained dental bridgework, and her husband never had such work done on him. (*Miami Herald*)

Residents of the town of Kazimierz Wielki, Poland, will be allowed a new suit of clothes only after they've died, the town council has decreed. That's so they can at least look respectable in the coffin. (*Daily Telegraph*)

One of the liveliest courses offered at Loyola Marymount University in Los Angeles is Dr Howard Delaney's course on death. Besides the required reading, students of his 'Philosophy of Death' course take field trips to mortuaries, to visit dying patients in nursing homes, to the UCLA Medical School to watch corpses being dissected, and to the County Coroner's office. They also must plan the funeral of a loved one, and they hold a mock funeral for Dr Delaney, who climbs into a coffin. The students' eulogies are full of praise for their 'beloved teacher'. All in all. 'There's a lot of laughter,' says Delaney, 'We use it to relieve tensions on field trips.' (*Los Angeles Herald-Examiner*)

Yugoslav kids are having some problems adjusting to the swinging life. The big hero in Yugoslavia these days is Tarzan, thanks to old Tarzan flicks, and the newspaper Politika *reports: 'Trees have been crowded with children, rooftops have become their targets, and everywhere one can hear cries imitating Tarzan.' Unfortunately, some of those jungle cries have become cries of another sort – doctors are reporting an epidemic of broken bones.* (Miami Herald)

Congratulations to Jessie Bryam of the Detroit suburb of Madison Heights on her graduation from high school with a straight 'A' record. Of course, she had the benefit of maturity. Bryam is 98 years old. She decided to pursue her high school diploma when some younger friends in their seventies, fellow residents at the Madison Heights Senior Citizens Centre, began taking courses. (*Chicago Tribune*)

The inhabitants of Madagascar don't forget the dead. Once every five or ten years, depending on when an astrologer says the time is right, they dig up the bones of old relatives to give them some fresh air and keep them posted on what's been going on. They take the bones around town, tell them the latest jokes, introduce them to new family members, hire bands to play for them and have feasts in their honour. Then they return them to their resting places. (*Los Angeles Times*)

There was panic in Austin, Texas, when a TV station broadcast a Hallowe'en Special entitled 'The Slime Creatures Invade Austin'. Emergency personnel reported they received about 125 phone calls from residents who feared they were in the slime creatures' path. (San Francisco Chronicle)

T. J. Stephenson has filed a $5,001 claim against Dade County, Florida, for depriving him of his car and the companionship of his dead dog 'Whisker' for three days. When the German Shepherd died eight months ago, Stephenson had him stuffed, and installed him in the back seat of his car, where he remained a faithful companion, until the day a passer-by saw the dead dog in the parked car, and phoned police, who hauled it off. (*Los Angeles Times*)

Scotland's newest novelty record is a scream. It's a song in praise of the school strap, entitled 'The Belt Has Got To Stay', and performed by the unlikeliest of singers – third-year pupils at Holy Cross School in Hamilton. The song was written by teachers Michael Toner and Graeme Liveston, in reaction to a decision by the European Court of Human Rights which could result in the banning of the strap in Scotland. Says Toner: 'I don't know what we would do without it. It is the only exercise that most teachers get.' As to how the teachers managed to induce their students to sing the strap's praises – one can only speculate. (*The Guardian*)

A study in West Germany finds that, for an increasing number of Germans, a speeding car is becoming the suicide method of choice. The study's author, Dr Werner Weber, of Aachen, estimates that 600 Germans a year, mainly men, are flooring their pedals and deliberately zooming to the end of their road. Swiss researcher Dr Alexander Balkanyi believes that this method appeals mainly to men because women are reluctant to mess up their looks, whereas a desperate man 'wants not only to destroy himself but also the car which he loves above all other things', in the manner of the classic tragedies where lovers end their lives together. Traffic psychologist Peter Seelmann suspects that a person might prefer to go out in a flaming crash 'to make headlines in order to give his relatives a guilty conscience'. He says that most of such crashes happen on straight-ahead freeways, where the driver has the chance to contemplate it all. (*The Times*)

There is an average of three guns per household in Gillette, Wyoming, or 15,000 guns altogether. That's the estimate of police chief Bob Hartman. But he says it's not a major problem. In 1981, there were only two murders in Gillette, and in only one was a gun used. (Denver Post)

Here is a product recall to note. The 'protecto hold me tite' squeeze toy is being recalled because infants may have choked to death while sucking on it, according to the Consumer Product Safety Commission. There are about 390,000 'protecto hold me tite' toys out there, in the form of pink elephants, yellow bears and orange lions. They can be returned to the point of purchase or mailed to Reliance Products, PO Box 1220, Woonsocket, RI. (*New York Times*)

Fate has played a dirty trick on civic boosters in Gillette, Wyoming. A campaign by the Gillette City Council to clean up the city's well-publicised image of being a grimy oil and coal boom town took a spill when more than 500 people became involved in a brawl at a mud-wrestling match. It started when someone pushed the match announcer into the mud-pit at the Boothill Bar, and police were called. Twenty police officers waded into the mêlée, which was also joined by the female mud-wrestlers. It was later revealed that the announcer's fall into the mud was all part of the show but that revelation came too late to wipe the new mud-stains off Gillette's image. (*Denver Post*)

If obesity is a health problem for Americans, it's even more of a problem with their pets. Veterinarians say that about 70 per cent of the dogs they see are overweight. The problem, says Springfield, Mass. veterinarian Richard Hersman, is that animals shamelessly hustle their owners for extra food when they're not even hungry, simply because 'they like to eat'. He says people kill 'their pets with kindness. They can't stand to see them beg or cry. It's just a good thing dogs can't smoke'. Hersman advises replacing portions of an overweight dog's food with cottage cheese or string beans, saying 'that gives them the same amount of bulk so they won't cry'. (New York Times)

A headline in the *South China Morning Post* read: 'Fisherman cheats death by drowning.' (*Punch*)

A candidate for San Francisco Board of Supervisors, who campaigned in a mini-skirted nun's habit, and listed his occupation as 'Nun of the Above' (spelled N-U-N), received almost 23,000 votes, finishing ninth in a field of twenty-four. There were only five seats up for grabs, but

'Sister Boom Boom' came close. Now she's discarded her political habit and revealed herself as 27-year-old Dick Fertig, a professional astrologer. Says Fertig: 'Going in drag has taught me a lot about the oppression of women. If every legislator had to wear heels, a corset, fake eyelashes and a zipper up the back, we'd have the equal rights amendment passed in a week.' His election showing was even better than the creditable vote count two years ago of Board of Supervisors Candidate Carl Lafonc, the Pastrami candidate, who campaigned for better delicatessen food, and banning the playing of disco music within 500 feet of any living thing. The worst election-day whipping in San Francisco this year was by Patrick Cimaroli, who took a bullwhip from beneath his white dress and began lashing an election worker at a polling place. He was arrested on charges of assault with a deadly weapon and interfering with an election. (*San Francisco Chronicle*; *Los Angeles Daily News*)

A Labour Party Parliamentary candidate has taken up the case of a mother and her three children who have had to climb out of a back window of their home for the last three years because their door is permanently locked. According to the politician, Martin Coleman, 25-year-old Mrs Berni Tyrell lost the door key three years ago, and her landlords, the City Housing Corporation in Northampton, don't keep duplicates. (Daily Telegraph)

A railwayman who tried to help a woman to board a train he had already signalled to start moving, only to see her fall and get run over, lost in his attempt to sue her estate for the emotional damage he suffered in witnessing the accident. Mrs Florence Fordham had both her legs severed when she fell between the platform and the train at the Dartford station. She died a year later of unrelated causes. 68-year-old Stanley May, who was a station foreman at the time but has since retired, told the court that he developed a nervous condition because of the accident. He claimed that Mrs Fordham was negligent in trying to board a moving train, and was supported in his suit by his union. But a High Court judge in London ruled that the railway employee was 95 per cent to blame for the mishap. He advised May and his wife to 'put the whole matter out of their minds'. (*Daily Telegraph*)

A 19-year-old Oceanside, California woman was simply lucky to be who she is, whoever that is – her identity wasn't released. She was sitting in a parked car waiting for her boyfriend when a man brandishing a knife jumped into the car, took a look at her and said: 'Wrong girl.' He told her to keep quiet and fled. Three bystanders chased and caught 20-year-old Daniel Barreto, of the nearby Camp Pendleton Marine Base, before he could find the right girl. (*San Diego Union*)

San Francisco's Golden Gate Bridge gets a four-star rating from the area's suicidal people. When it comes to ending it all, the Golden Gate Bridge has a definite jump on the nearby San Francisco–Oakland Bay Bridge, according to a recent study by Richard Seiden, a Professor of Behavioral Sciences at University of California – Berkeley's School of Public Health. Seiden concludes that style-conscious suicides consider using the Bay Bridge to be 'tacky', whereas the Golden Gate Bridge is 'aesthetically pleasing'. The Golden Gate Bridge, says Seiden, 'has developed into a kind of suicide shrine – a place where people could end their lives with grace and beauty'. (Los Angeles Times)

A North London man who spent close to £270,000 of money donated by or borrowed from the faithful to proclaim, in big newspaper ads around the world, that

Christ would be appearing on the scene within two months, now concedes that the Second Coming was something of a non-event. Benjamin Creme had said that the New Christ was a Pakistani native living in East London. Now that more than two months have gone by, the 59-year-old Creme blames Christ's non-appearance on the scepticism of the press, which failed to pursue 'The Story of the Century'. Had the press used its investigative resources, he says, Christ would have been located. For now what bothers him is the number of people who come knocking on his door and phoning him, announcing that they are Christ. Says Creme: 'They are cranks, just cranks.' (*Sunday Express*)

A prosecutor in San José, California, has proposed a stiff sentence to fit the crime committed by 19-year-old Brent A. Jones. Jones was convicted on a misdemeanor count of disturbing remains after he was nailed opening a casket at the Gates of Heaven Cemetery in nearby Los Altos. He explained that he just wanted to see a dead body. Santa Clara County Superior Court Judge Conrad Rushing was ready to sentence Jones to thirty days in jail, when Prosecutor Alan Nudelman used his noodle to dig up a proposal for a stiffer sentence – a stint in the County Coroner's Office. Said the Prosecutor: 'He wants to see a dead body? We'll show him some dead bodies.' The Judge delayed sentence until 8 September to consider it. (*Los Angeles Herald-Examiner*)

An outbreak of peace in West Beirut resulted in at least three deaths and at least forty people being hospitalised. The casualties were caused by stray or falling bullets, as Moslems fired their guns in the air in a celebration saluting the departing Palestinian fighters. (New York Times)

Authorities in Papua New Guinea are concerned by an increase in casualties resulting from tribal fighting in the Highlands region. The tribesmen have been going at it for centuries, generally over pigs and women, but the recent introduction of new, more modern weapons has raised the toll of dead and injured. Up until recently, they fought with stone and wooden weapons, but now they've started using steel axes and spears. (Reuters, *Los Angeles Times*)

Although India is struggling itself, its Government is still willing at times to lend a helping hand to others. In the latest humanitarian move, India's industry ministry has confirmed that it will lend assistance to Ayatollah Khomeini's Government, to help the Iranian Mullahs develop nuclear power. (*Sacramento Bee*)

Some people were disturbed to see Ralph Cone and his wife walking down a downtown San Diego street with a 5-foot snake wrapped around the baby Cone was carrying. When one man asked Cone if the snake was dangerous, he didn't reply directly, but instead pulled out a switchblade and tried to slash the man. The two parents then resumed their leisurely stroll, amusing themselves by tossing the snake-wrapped baby back and forth. Police charged Cone with several misdemeanours. The snake, which turned out to be harmless, was placed in an animal shelter. The baby wasn't as lucky – it went back to its parents. (San Diego Union)

A 96-year-old New York woman has filed a suit in Manhattan, claiming that she was tricked into signing over to her granddaughter two four-storey brownstone buildings she owned in Greenwich Village. Reba Morse says she had been invited to a friend's apartment, and arrived to find her son, her granddaughter, three lawyers, a notary and a psychiatrist. They convinced her to sign some papers, which, she says, they told her was simply a way to reduce her taxes. She says she only found out that the two buildings, including one she lives in, were no longer hers when her granddaughter demanded the first month's rent – $3,600. But at least she didn't ask for first and last month's rent. (*St Louis Post-Dispatch*)

'My baby, my baby, save my baby,' Marie Higuera screamed hysterically as she stood outside her burning home in Portland, Oregon. Tony Stellato of Scappoose, Oregon was there to answer her pleas. He had been driving home from work when he saw the burning house. Hearing her scream about her baby, he rushed into the house and searched until the flames and smoke drove him out. But she screamed again, so he charged back in. Stellato later said, 'I was scared and I don't know what came over me, but I had amazing strength. I broke right through a door.' But he got hit by a surge of smoke, and barely made it outside before he passed out. He was revived by firefighters and hospitalised for smoke inhalation. He asked a nurse there about the baby. That's when he was told that the woman was referring to her cat. The good news was – the cat managed to escape on its own. (*Portland Oregonian*)

A coroner's jury in Brampton, Ontario has recommended that ambulance workers are not allowed to work more than twelve hours a day. The jurors were moved to this conclusion after an ambulance attendant in Mississauga, near Toronto, testified that he didn't try to revive a man who had suffered a fatal heart attack, because he was too tired. 46-year-old James O'Neill, who had a long history of heart problems, collapsed while jogging. The attendant, 36-year-old Tom Colpitts, who later resigned, said he didn't try to resuscitate O'Neill at the scene or on the way to the hospital because he was 'extremely tired, both mentally and physically' from working 16-hour shifts two consecutive days. Nurses at the hospital testified that they were shocked at the attendant's inaction. (Toronto Star)

According to a study in the most recent *New England Journal of Medicine*, people who were asked whether they would choose surgery if they had lung cancer gave differing answers, depending on how the question was put. People told there was a 90 per cent chance of survival were more likely to choose surgery than those told there was a 10 per cent chance of death. (*Los Angeles Herald-Examiner*)

People who administer mouth-to-mouth resuscitation are warned to first clear the victims' throats, and they should also clear their own, warn doctors at White Memorial Medical Centre in Los Angeles. They cite the case of a man who collapsed at a reception and was revived mouth-to-mouth by a bartender. The man later developed throat pains and breathing difficulties. On the man's sixth day in the hospital, doctors finally discovered the reason – the bartender had deposited his dental bridge in the man's throat. (*San Francisco Chronicle*)

What, you're running out of exposed areas of your skin on which to stick your jewellery? Well, my dear, maybe it's time you had your fingernails pierced. At Keirnan's Nail-N-Skin Etc. Shop in Sacramento, California, Carol Keirnan charges $50 and upwards to drill a hole in the fingernail, suitable for inserting a diamond, ruby or birthstone (Entrepreneur Magazine)

Another male chauvinist stronghold has fallen in California, in a hail of bullets. The California Highway Patrol is now using female silhouettes, as well as male silhouettes, as targets on its shooting ranges. Says CHP

Academy Commander, Capt Bill Carlson: 'We're not trying to teach our officers to shoot women.' Rather, the idea is to make it easier on officers when they do have to shoot a woman, which is happening more often, since 'women are shooting officers more often'. To avoid accusations of sexism, the silhouettes are given a very modest build and costume – no buxom women in hot-pants here. (*San Francisco Chronicle*)

In the past five years, more than 10,000 people have dropped in on Maria and Eduardo Rubio in Lake Arthur, New Mexico. But it's not the Rubios they want to see so much as their tortilla. It all started on 5 October 1977, when the face of Jesus appeared on the tortilla as it was sizzling in a skillet. The tortilla is now enshrined in the living room. (*Los Angeles Daily News*)

A 15-year-old glue-sniffing addict who was sent off to a government-run treatment centre in Sheffield emerged looking like a punk, his mother complains. Mrs Elaine Jepson of Rotherham says that the Keppel View Centre bought her boy, Carl, white leopard-skin trousers, punk shoes, and a ripped T-shirt. (The Times)

Be careful about using a fur sleeping bag when camping out. The fur bags are liable to get holes in them. Bullet holes. That's what happened to 22-year-old Manfred Koberle's fur sleeping bag. The German tourist was visiting the Italian island of Elba. He was shot dead in his sleep by a man who mistook him for a wild boar (*The Times*)

The Cambodian Government is showing some respect for the abilities of the nation's women. The official government radio reports that the Cambodian Government is using units of women to deactivate land mines in Svay

Rieng Province, bordering Vietnam. In five days of operations, the women were reported to have recovered 56 mines and 1,243 sharp pieces of iron and bamboo that had been buried. (*Los Angeles Times*)

The inmates of Askham Grange Prison in North Yorkshire were so sorry to see their warden leave that they threw a surprise party for him and his wife. After two years as the first male warden at the women's prison, Joe Whitty has been promoted to a men's prison. He was so well liked at Askham Grange that nobody tried to escape. Said one woman inmate of his departure: 'We're all heart-broken.' Said Whitty: 'They're a good lot really.' (The Guardian)

Doctors at Northwestern Memorial Hospital in Chicago chased and caught a man who had snatched a diamond ring from the finger of a patient, and managed to recover the ring, but only after some bloody knifework. They grabbed the ring from the stomach of 25-year-old Melvin Riddell, in an operation, after X-rays had located it. (*Chicago Sun-Times*)

Chartered buses full of old people have been banned from stopping at a Berkeley pub, the Huntsman House Inn. Pub owner Martin Riley says the old folks were stealing too many glasses, bottles and ash trays. (*Daily Telegraph*)

There's a real flowering of creativity, among people who owe money, says Les Kirschbaum, Head of a Morton Grove, Illinois collection agency – the Mid-Continent Adjustment Co. One man placed his own obituary in a paper and mailed clippings to his creditors. A woman said she ran over her husband with a car, leaving him with two broken arms and unable to write cheques for three months. Another woman said she was on the way to the post office to mail her cheques when she slipped and lost them in the snow, but she'd retrieve them in the spring. One flower-shop owner was more upbeat, she said she had to wait for people to die to earn her money, but 'we expect business to pick up in several weeks'. (*Los Angeles Times*)

Snow White wasn't lily-pure enough for the members of the First Assembly of God Church in Texas City. Snow White *was among the books, records and figurines ripped and smashed to bits as satanic in a ceremony of purification. Other Walt Disney fairy tales that mention witches met the same fate. They had originally planned to toss them all in a big bonfire, but the devil sent rain on the day in question.* (Portland Oregonian)

Things got pretty crazy at the North Bay Psychiatric Hospital in North Bay, Ontario, an Ontario legislature health committee was told. For six months, the 280-bed psychiatric facility went without a full-time psychiatrist on the staff. 'Doctors don't want to come to such an isolated area,' said Dr John Deadman, acting Chief of Staff, 'and even if they do come . . . the burnout is very high because there's so much work to do'. (*Toronto Star*)

A judge in Cowansville, Quebec, has taken steps to ensure that Jean-Luc Bonneau, age 47, will be a whole new person when he completes his sentence for indecently assaulting two boys. The judge sentenced Bonneau to three years of treatment with female hormones, in order to cure his sexual appetite. He also ordered a cure for Bonneau's alcoholism and gave him twenty months in prison. (*Toronto Star*)

The foreign country with the most burning demand for American flags is undoubtedly Iran. US flags are a hot item in Iran. They go through quite a few of them. But it's a mystery where they're getting all their American flags. A Christian Science Monitor *investigation finds the major flag companies in America denying that they would sell to the Iranians, because, as the head of one firm says:* 'We know how they're going to end up.' *A State Department spokesman thinks they must be making them in Iran.* (Christian Science Monitor)

As part of its never-ending battle against satanic influences, Iran's special Court of War on Sins has ordered a ban on church organ music, according to Iranian exile sources in London. But they say that church leaders intend to keep the music playing. (*San Francisco Chronicle*)

A wild buffalo that had been wreaking havoc with traffic around Victoria Falls in Zimbabwe finally met its match. The buffalo had been charging cars and carts for several days, but picked the wrong target when it charged a moving train head-on. It was killed instantly. (*Los Angeles Times*)

The Iranian Government has announced that a 14-year-old boy has been appointed Mayor of the town of Zobaydat, Iraq, which was captured by Iranian forces on 7 November. Although of tender years, the lad is a seasoned combat veteran. (The Times)

New York City's campaign to crack down on subway cheaters who go through the turnstiles using cheaper Connecticut turnpike tokens similar to the subway tokens has undergone a name change. It was known as 'Operation Leper', but has been changed to 'Operation Pariah' after complaints from lepers and leprosy groups. (*Los Angeles Times*)

Money is the root of all evil. That was demonstrated when fighting involving knives and clubs erupted at the Syrian Orthodox Church in the Sydney, Australia suburb of Lidcombe, triggered by a dispute over who would pass the collection plate. (*Brisbane Courier-Mail* in *Punch*)

Mr and Mrs Gordon Craddock are fed up with uninvited visitors who crash in on them in Surrey. Ten times in the last five years, cars have smashed through their fence, ploughed through flower beds and torn up the lawn. It's a tricky curve. Mr 'Crash' Craddock has been trying, unsuccessfully so far, to get county officials to erect a crash barrier. (Sunday Express)

A Windsor, Ontario man who indecently assaulted a hospital patient who was hooked up to intravenous and other tubes has been sentenced to six months in jail. The court was told that William Weathers, a 22-year-old parolee, had been drinking at the time of the assault, but that he is now enrolled in five university courses. (*Toronto Globe & Mail*)

Church officials were aware that 35-year-old Robert Green was a convicted rapist and sex offender when they hired him as a helper at the Baptist Youth Club in Braintree, Essex. But they felt that Green had already been punished, and it was not fair to punish him again. Now he has to take at least a temporary absence from his youth club job. He's been sentenced to six years in jail after pleading guilty to indecently assaulting three young girls. (*Daily Telegraph*)

Health officials in Edmonton, Alberta are waiting for the real cold weather to hit, in December, to conduct further tests of the phenomenon known as 'bingo brain'. A case of bingo brain, involving a woman who developed symptoms of wooziness and confusion, had been reported in the British Medical Journal. *It's thought that all the smoke in bingo halls caused carbon monoxide poisoning. When the bitter cold causes all of Edmonton's bingo hall windows to be closed, the authorities will perform some checks.* (Toronto Globe & Mail)

North Korean health vice-minister Li Jong Ryul blames the death of South Korean boxer Duk Koo Kim on 'US imperialist murderers' who, 'while pretending to give treatment' to the unconscious boxer, 'plotted to remove his heart and kidneys'. (*Los Angeles Times*)

The Centre for Disease Control in Atlanta reports that 80,000 people are dying annually from infections caught in hospitals. (*Denver Post*)

Take it off

MEN – when you take off your clothes, does your lover look bored? There could be something missing in your strip act. A how-to book to be out in August may be what you need. *Take It Off* by Jacques Toulouse is billed as a do-it-yourself guide to home stripping, offering 'All you need to know about taking off your clothes'. It's illustrated with 120 informative photos that will take you step by step. (*Chicago Tribune*)

A worldwide survey of religious relics by the Italian newspaper *Republica*, which took years to draw up an inventory of all relics that could be traced, has turned up some miraculous findings. They indicate that many of the saints were even more remarkable than had been supposed. For instance, the newspaper found ten skulls of St John the Baptist, the apostle James left behind nine heads and eighteen arms, and St George, the English patron saint, left behind enough bones to make up thirty complete skeletons. (*Sunday Express*)

Survival Tomorrow, *a newsletter for people who want to save their skins from a nuclear war, has published a new list of 'Best Bets' where people can go to survive a holocaust. They include Hawaii, New Zealand, and parts of Appalachia. Gone from the list is an old favourite 'Best Bet' – The Falkland Islands.* (Wall St Journal)

The Australian Institute of Petroleum is investigating a chemical which could reduce petrol sniffing in Aboriginal communities. The Aborigines are getting high on the fumes which can cause brain damage if inhaled regularly. A spokesman for the Institute said, 'The odorant is placed in petrol drums and has a skunklike smell which causes nausea if inhaled in large quantities.' (*The Australian Advertiser*)

An alarm for coffins, which sounds a beeper if the deceased comes back to life, has been unveiled at the International Inventors Exposition in New York. Roberto Monsivais of Mexico City developed what he calls 'The Life Detector'. It features monitoring equipment connected to an alarm, and also an oxygen supply to keep the revived person from slipping back to the other side, until he can be dug out of the ground. (*Sacramento Bee*)

A Japanese company has come up with canned sweat. No, this isn't some novelty joke item. It's a beverage, named 'Sweat', which is described as a 'health-oriented drink which supplies water and electrolytes lost through perspiration'. (Gallery; Chicago Tribune)

Democracy of a sort has come to China's elementary schools. Whereas, formerly, only youngsters considered politically advanced were allowed to join the Communist Young Pioneers, now all students are to become members. (*New York Times*)

Sometimes it can be a small world indeed. A bottle with a message in it that was thrown into the ocean at Winterton, England in 1959 has been found, some twenty-three years later ... at Winterton, England. (*Eastern Daily Press*, in *Punch*)

A Canadian criminologist believes that the answer to overcrowded prisons will be prison colonies in space. Dr Ezzat Fattah, of Simon Fraser University in Vancouver, says: 'It seems entirely possible that the first permanent inhabitants in space will be criminals.' As long as they don't reach escape velocity. (Today Magazine)

Here's mud in your eye and all over your skin, at $12.95 for a 2-ounce bottle of the thick, slimy black goo. 'It's one of the very few things I can say is truly 100 per cent natural,' says Mario Ebanietti, President of the Cosmetest Corp, an East Rutherford, New Jersey cosmetics firm that's acquired exclusive American rights to market this special mud from the Dead Sea. Test-marketing in New York and New Jersey will begin in September. The mud is said to be rich in healthful minerals like magnesium, potassium and sodium, and West Germans are reportedly big on it for ailments like arthritis, psoriasis and tired blood. Ebanietti, however, doesn't want to promote it as a magical muck. He simply says: 'It relaxes the skin and it's great for cleansing the hair.' (*Wall St Journal*)

Advances in computer technology and neuroscience will enable even the most non-psychic people to communicate by mental telepathy by early in the next century. That's according to Dr Glenn Cartwright of McGill University's Computer-Based Instructional Research Lab in Montreal. He says: 'The idea is no more incredible than had I suggested a hundred years ago that we were going to project human voices around the world.' Tiny microprocessor chips implanted in each brain will enable people to hook up mentally with a huge central computer to which everyone else will be connected, he says. And, since the computer will possess every bit of codable information in the world, and be able to transmit directly into the brain, everybody will become know-it-alls. Dr Cartwright says that a Rockville, Maryland firm, E.M.V. Associates, is developing the protein components that could be used to make an organic microchip suitable for placement in the brain. (*Science Digest*)

A heart pacemaker has been successfully implanted in Henri Perignon, a resident of Caen, France. Perignon is 102 years old. He had been complaining that he was getting short of breath while engaging in his favourite sport – cycling. (The Guardian)

Probably the dullest telephone hotline in existence has been started up in New York. The recorded voice is so dull, it's liable to put the caller to sleep, which is the intention. 'Sleepline', as it's called, is operated by Lenox Hill Hospital as a service for insomniacs. The voice is that of a doctor who uses hypnotic techniques to help people doze off. (*Wall St Journal*)

The newsletter of the Syon Mission Church in Brentford announces this upcoming event: 16 December – A visit to heaven. Venue to be announced.' (*Daily Telegraph*)

According to official Russian Government figures, in a period of two weeks beginning 24 May, 48 million Russians attended some 14,000 peace rallies sponsored by the official Soviet Peace Committee. There's no arguing over attendance figures; the rallies are so well organised that the crowd size is often announced in advance. A *Daily Telegraph* reporter who attended one such rally in a Moscow stadium says he had to flash his press card before rally stewards would allow him to leave early. (*Daily Telegraph*)

Contrary to earlier reports, a Soviet Armenian newspaper reports that the worker whose parents named him 'Fulfil

74

the five-year-plan in four' is not at all happy with the name. He'd like to change it, but is worried about how that would look in the eyes of Soviet authorities. They might question his dedication. (New York Times)

Japanese golfers can now buy insurance protection against one of golf's biggest hazards in that country – a hole-in-one. A \$4 annual premium will purchase \$2,000 worth of hole-in-one insurance coverage, sufficient to pay the cost of the celebration the unfortunate golfer is expected to lay on. The first to collect was 68-year-old Shuzo Babazono, head of an iron factory. (*Weekend Australian*)

Democrats in New Mexico are trying to bring down Republican Senator Harrison Schmitt, a former astronaut, by posing the campaign question: 'What on earth has he done?' (*Wall St Journal*)

Computers will be installed in all of Sweden's alcohol stores which are government run, to indicate if would-be buyers have already had enough to drink, if a bill in the Swedish Parliament passes. Under the bill, introduced by Member of Parliament Marianne Carlsson of the ruling Centre Party, liquor buyers would have to produce a booze identity card with a number that would be fed into a computer terminal. If the buyer's order put him or her over a certain allowed quantity of alcohol, a red light would flash on the computer within seconds. Customers who repeatedly got red lights might have to undergo compulsory treatment. (*Sunday Express*)

Here's the perfect gift to give people who say they only drink alcohol for medicinal purposes. The Hawkeye Distilling Co. of Skokie, Illinois has introduced a new live-giving vodka, 'Mash 4077', 4077 being the hospital *unit number in the TV show 'Mash'. The beverage comes in an intravenous feeding bottle, complete with a 17-inch stand and a silicon hose. At $20 for a 1-litre bottle, it's the kind of thing you'd want to save for an emergency. But, hey, how can you put a price on your life?* (People Magazine)

A small San Francisco Bay area radio station has gained a loyal late-night audience by playing the latest of the new waves. Listeners tuning into 'Kmah', a low-power station in Menlo Park, California, between the hours of 10 pm and 7.30 am simply hear the roar of the Pacific Ocean, the crashing of waves against the shore, and an occasional foghorn. Since this new easy-listening programming began four months ago, the station has received a steady flow of appreciative comments from listeners who say the late-night show puts them to sleep beautifully, or helps them to study better. 'The only problem', says General Manager Frank Spinetta, 'is keeping the person awake who has to sit here all night.' (*Sacramento Bee*)

Do couples who have been married forty years or more need lessons on how to talk to each other? They most certainly do, says Marsha Bollendorf. She's offering workshops on 'starting over: couple communication for the newly retired' through the college of Du Page in the Chicago suburb of Glen Ellyn, Illinois. She says that retirement means that marriage partners who have managed largely to avoid each other for decades must suddenly learn how to have conversations. (*Chicago Sun-Times*)

Researchers at the University of California-San Diego came across a startling discovery – the more money you have, the better you sleep. At least that applied to residents of the wealthy San Diego suburb of La Jolla

(Joya) who were studied. According to the researchers, those residents were generally 'very satisfied with their sleep patterns'. But, for wealthy people who do lie awake with worries, a San Francisco company has the answer. It's selling mink teddy bears, for $160 each. (Intro Magazine; Wall Street Journal)

A Los Angeles Republican Congressional candidate proposed his own get-tough-on-crime programme. Howard D. Felsher suggests jailing all teenagers, before they have a chance to commit a crime. He wrote in a newsletter: '(It's) a harsh and startling thought perhaps, but our young people must be shown the realities of modern living.' He suggests mandatory three-day jail sentences for every high school graduate. It would give them a taste of life behind bars, and eliminate any nasty ideas they might be entertaining. 'Nothing has worked in 2,000 years,' he says, 'so we should try something new.' (*Los Angeles Daily News*)

Forty thousand residents of India commit suicide every year, according to a government study. The most frequent reason is agony due to disease. The second major cause of suicide in India is 'quarrels with parents-in-law'. (*San Francisco Chronicle*)

When it comes to accepting that they have cancer, doctors make the most difficult patients of all, says psychiatrist Dr Robert Taubman of the Oregon Health Sciences Centre in Portland. He told a recent American psychiatric association meeting in Toronto: 'Doctors have a massive denial of life-threatening illnesses', because 'they're supposed to be invincible and immortal, and become very angry if illness befalls them.' Taubman suggests that medical schools include instruction on how to be a patient. (*Chicago Tribune*)

Hoegh Industries, the nation's largest manufacturer of pet coffins, now offers them in twenty styles, including customised caskets for skunks, snakes, chickens, monkeys, mice and ducks. (Entrepreneur Magazine)

Worship has been computerised at St Thomas's Church in Birmingham. A modern computer now plans the services, selects the hymns ('The Lord is my Programmer'?) and teaches Bible and Sunday School classes. It also does the books. (*The Times*)

The marijuana harvest had the atmosphere of a church social in Newcastle, Oklahoma, as a hundred volunteers, recruited through area churches, sang hymns as they helped gather the crop, and were fed cookies and lemonade. They had to agree not to keep any for themselves. It was simply to help the cops, who had discovered the 10-acre field. (*St Louis Post-Dispatch*)

Christmas came early for the former Winfred Eugene Holley, as he was granted a legal name change to 'Santa Claus'. But then Christmas is an all-year-round thing for the 63-year-old cheery fellow with the white beard and red shirt. Los Angeles Superior Court Commissioner Bertrand D. Mouron Jr, who granted the change, said: 'I was expecting some kind of nut twitching around, but . . . he absolutely radiates Santa Clausness.' (Los Angeles Times)

A Federal jury in Los Angeles has convicted of mail fraud two promoters who milked investors for millions of dollars in unrepaid loans for their plan to produce inexpensive auto fuel from solar cells. Prosecutors told the court that, among other things, Gerald Schaflander and Stephen Wright boasted that their solar-powered car made two cross-country runs. What they failed to add was that it was towed most of the way. (*Los Angeles Times*)

Parents are handicapping their children by not teaching them how to lie, says a self-proclaimed expert on lying, psychiatrist Harold A. Rashkis. Rashkis, who practises in Elkins Park, Pennsylvania, and also at the University of Pennsylvania Hospital in Philadelphia, admits that 'lying is one of my favourite topics' – except that he'd rather call it 'the politics of living'. He says little children grow up with an unreasonable fear of lying because they think their parents are omnipotent and can detect any lies. The youngster then grows up to carry these irrational fears into adult situations where lying might be needed – for instance, a job interview. Rashkis urges parents to teach their children how to stonewall, bluff and fake, and convey to them that they can get away with it. (*Chicago Tribune*)

Lockheed Missiles and Space Co. is using carrier pigeons daily to transport microfilms of computer print-outs from headquarters in Sunnyvale, California, to its test base in Santa Cruz. That's a journey of twenty-two miles as the bird flies, but fifty miles by truck along winding mountain roads. Werner Deeg, who manages the pigeons, says that using the birds is much cheaper and quicker than trucking the print-outs, and considerably cheaper than transmitting them electronically. He says that although the birds aren't used in bad weather, when they are used their reliability is 100 per cent. (Wall St Journal)

Twelve thousand Americans were injured falling off bar stools, or impacting with the stools in some way, in the year ending 30 June, according to a survey of injuries treated in hospital emergency rooms. The survey has just been released by the Consumer Product Safety Commission.

Another 110,000 were injured by drinking glasses, and another 26,000 were hurt dancing. Steps, ramps and landings led the way as the cause of injuries, with 763,000 unfortunates having been hurt on them, or falling off them. Chairs and sofas claimed a toll of 236,000 injuries. And, for those who think they'd have been better off staying in bed – well, 199,000 people were injured in or around beds. (*New York Times*)

A *Reader's Digest* science writer is advocating the banning of a newly discovered chemical, which, he says, could be used by politicians to make themselves more lovable. Lowell Ponte says that the body chemical androsterone, which is found in the sweat of pigs, politicians and humans in small amounts, acts as a sex attractant for pigs, but in humans it seems to have a social function, augmenting the attractiveness of a leader. He says experimental subjects at the University of Birmingham in England who inhaled a vapour of androsterone described people in photographs as more attractive and interesting than they had before. Ponte fears that politicians could spray the chemical in aerosol form at political rallies, or use it in the ink of their campaign literature. Since it is hard to detect, he says, 'You would never notice that you were being led around, literally, by the nose.' (*San Francisco Chronicle*)

What, you stocked your wine cellar with red wines, only to find that white wine is now the 'in' beverage? No problem. The Corning Glass Co. has announced the development of an enzyme that turns red wine into white. (Entrepreneur Magazine)

Canada's Agriculture Department is turning into a soft touch for the country's dairy farmers. The Department has announced the allocation of $112,000 for a study on how to improve the 'spreadability' of butter. Before taxpayers heat up, the Department explains that butter consumption is declining because it is so hard to spread. (*Toronto Globe & Mail*)

The next hot fabric in the textile industry, say the fashion rag *Daily News Record*, will be a fabric that is resistant to biological and chemical warfare. 'Money is no problem,' says Col Peter Hidalgo of the US Army Chemical School in Fort McClellan, Alabama, 'every member of the armed forces needs at least one of these uniforms'. And soon the general public may feel the same way. (*Chicago Tribune*)

Women looking for a man of the strong, silent, non-smoking, non-drinking variety might want to contact Mildred Huie of St Simons Island, Georgia. She can fix you up with a real doll. The 75-year-old widow is turning out life-sized male dolls, broad-shouldered and well dressed, for single women who want to be seen with a male companion, for safety or other reasons. The 'man for all seasons' doll is yours for $150. (Sacramento Bee)

The Social Security Administration has agreed to alter official letters that critics charged were confusing people. The letters informed recipients that their disability benefits were being cut off, and were headed: 'Notice of Favourable Decision'. The favourable aspect was that the person being terminated would not have to repay benefits already received. (*Los Angeles Times*)

Wily robbers in Meaux, France, held up the local post office and made an easy getaway with 244,000 francs in loot, without much worry of being chased. Before pulling the job, they had padlocked the gates to the police parking lot. (*Daily Telegraph*)

A man who slept through a four-hour police siege of his home was finally awakened by his sister bellowing through a bullhorn, a Manchester court was told. Police went to 35-year-old Roy Wilson's home after concerned neighbours reported that his family had not been seen for several days. As it turned out his wife had left him and the kids were staying elsewhere. At one point, a plain-clothes policeman climbed through a window, but Wilson apparently thought he was a burglar and chased him off with an imitation gun, then went back to sleep. (Daily Telegraph)

A 29-year-old psychotic man with a history of hearing imaginary voices, was cured when he was given a set of stereo headphones, reports psychiatrist Robert Feder of Yale University. Now he still hears crazy voices, but they belong to real-life radio announcers. (*American Journal of Psychiatry*)

Gambling addicts quite often go through withdrawal symptoms, according to a report in the *British Journal of Addiction*. These symptoms may include mood swings, anxiety attacks, nausea, the shakes, chest pains and muscle cramps. (*Chicago Tribune*)

The Russian Communist Party Central Committee has decided that the late Leonid Brezhnev's memory will be imbedded in concrete. It's announced that a huge cement plant will be named after the late leader, as well as a metallurgical plant, a number of other factories, a dam, a tank division, a city of 300,000, and districts in Moscow and in Brezhnev's home town. (Los Angeles Times)

Many would probably feel that there are more unpleasant instances of police brutality than the attack reported by Patrick G. Lamoureux of Seattle. The 25-year-old tree-trimmer charged that he was at work on a tree near the waterfront when he was physically set upon by a female police officer wearing only a bikini. Lamoureux alleged that Officer Theresa L. Martin pulled his hair and 'put an arm lock' on him, then walked away. For this, she was suspended for three days without pay. Now Lamoureux has filed a suit against the city for unspecified damages as the result of this traumatic incident. (*Portland Oregonian*)

Autumn leaves are causing a lot of delays for trains in Sweden. Swedish rail executives have had to explain to upset passengers that the new $70 million electronic safety system is able to detect objects on the tracks, including leaves, and automatically causes train brakes to jam before the train strikes such obstacles, thereby avoiding a rail disaster. Railway spokesman Kuell-Olof Forslind admits that the company has been spending a fortune replacing locomotive wheels damaged by all these screeching stops. (*Sunday Express*)

Most airlines are cutting back on frills, but when Firstair of Los Angeles starts flying next spring, service will be first class to say the least, and the firm expects business to take off. The line plans to start with flights between Los Angeles and New York, LA and Honolulu, and New York and Miami, with each flight accommodating only twenty passengers, in a living-room type atmosphere. There will be tables, lamps, a restaurant, a manicurist, a hairdresser, a secretary, a copy machine, a stock ticker and four conference rooms. Firstair won't be joining the price war that has seen some LA–New York fares drop below $100. For that trip, it will charge $1,500. (Sacramento Bee)

The Japanese–American firm Epson America has joined with the Landmark Limousine Company of Woodland

Hills, California to produce what's billed as the 'limousine of the future'. It's a stretched-out white Mercedes equipped with desktop computer, another portable computer, an electronic foot massage, a towel warmer, a clothes steamer, a battery-operated shoe shiner, a stereo, a nail dryer, a telephone, an air-pressurised bar, an assortment of exercise equipment, a pulse tracker and a smokeless ashtray. The price tag on this loaded-with-options limo is $150,000. (*Los Angeles Times*)

Chicago-based *Jet* magazine reports on a Chicago man waiting for a subway train who tried to show some friends how you can tell whether a train's approaching. He jumped on to the tracks and put his ear to a rail. Unfortunately, he put his ear to the third rail, in what turned out to be too hot an idea, and was electrocuted. (*Jet Magazine*)

The Skyway Luggage Co. of Seattle has come up with some handy tips for the travelling executive who finds his wardrobe spotted or wrinkled before a big meeting. A spot on a dark suit or tie can be instantly masked by applying some black coffee. On lighter fabrics, club soda works. A felt-tip marker can rid dark shoes of scuffs. Wrinkles can be taken out of a tie, shirt or blouse by rubbing it with a hot light bulb. And if an iron but no ironing board is available, a toilet seat makes an ideal substitute. (Los Angeles Times)

Onion-flavoured milk is the only way to go for Algerian babies. The tots rejected a NICEF-developed protein drink until International Flavours and Fragrances, a Hazlet, New Jersey firm that specialises in making scents, came to the rescue with an onion-flavoured additive that imitated the milk of Algerian mothers. Among the company's many other achievements have been a tobacco flavouring for low-tar-and-nicotine cigarettes, an aerosol aroma of baked bread for a Cincinnati bakery that was losing business because of the smell of a nearby pizza joint, and an aroma of 'essence of slum' for a Smithsonian exhibit. That one included a hint of the scents of rubbish and urine. (*Fortune Magazine*)

A couple in Cleveland, Ohio found a wallet containing $65 and a $300 money order, and returned it to the rightful owner. Names of the pair were not released, for their own protection. They asked a newspaper not to publish their names, out of fear they would be ridiculed for returning the money. The two, identified only as 'Ron' and 'Helen', said they had read of another man who was harassed and ridiculed after he returned a large sum of money he found. (*Sacramento Bee*)

The Emperor Napoleon was indeed having problems by the time he faced the Battle of Waterloo. Not only was he losing his hold on his Empire, but the Emperor himself was becoming an Empress, against his will. That's the speculation of endocrine expert Dr Robert Greenblatt, writing in the Journal of Sexual Medicine. *He feels that Napoleon was suffering from a rare hormonal disorder that was gradually turning him into a woman. That would account for his problem: urinating during the siege of Moscow, his violent stomach pains at Dresden, the swollen legs at Borodia, and the lethargy and piles he suffered at Waterloo. Physicians who conducted a post-mortem examination on Napoleon noted the general feminisation of his body. Said one: 'He had a chest that many a woman would envy', as well as shrunken genitals.* (The Guardian)

Researchers at the Australian Government's Commonwealth Scientific and Industrial Research Organisation have come up with a way to shear sheep without the sheer labour. Simply inject a natural substance, epidermal growth factor, and the wool falls off. It later grows back. (*Science 82*)

As if acid rain isn't enough of a cause for concern already, a group of Dutch scientists have fingered cow manure as a significant contributor to the acid rain problem. Dr N. van Breemen and colleagues at the Agricultural University in Wageningen say that the reeking ammonia which rises from liquid manure combines with sulphur dioxide to create fine white crystals of ammonium sulphate that settle on all available surfaces, especially trees. They are later washed into the soil. (*Nature Magazine*)

Left-handed police officers in Brussels, Belgium can now be quicker on the draw. The even-handed town council has voted to spend $6,000 on special left-handed holsters. Previously, lefties had to draw with the right hand and then flip the gun to the left hand before shooting. (San Francisco Chronicle)

A vacuum cleaner that also cuts hair is being offered by the Kirby division of Cleveland's Scott & Fetzer Co. and it certainly helps get rid of dandruff. (*Wall Street Journal*)

According to the *Wharton* magazine, the latest in bullet-proof wear includes bullet-proof umbrellas, and, for the harried housewife, or the butcher who doesn't want his apron bloodier than necessary, bullet-proof aprons. (*Chicago Tribune*)

William L. Jellison of Hamilton, Montana has been trying without success for twenty years to get rid of his fleas. He has 2,000 of them. The retired scientist who once did flea research for the government has amassed an impressive collection of fleas from animals ranging from dead grizzlies and mountain lions to skunks and squirrels, but he hasn't been able to find a university or museum that wants the fleas. He says: 'It's a challenge to get rid of this stuff.' (*Wall Street Journal*)

They are on the job night and day

HAVE you hugged a vending machine today? This week (24–31 October) is 'Hug a Vending Machine Week', under the auspices of the National Automatic Merchandising Association. William Buckholz, a Reading, Pennsylvania vending company owner who originated the slogan, says 'They are on the job night and day, yet no one ever gives them a pat on the back.' People do hug his machines, but even there he has to bribe them with an offer of a free drink or candy bar. (*Los Angeles Times*)

In case of a nuclear attack, the US Government has this advice for evacuees, do not – repeat, do not – leave home without your credit cards. They will be honoured after an attack. However, survivalist Duncan Long recommends carrying along penicillin, candy and .22 calibre bullets. He says they'll be the most valuable items for trading purposes. (Newsweek)

An American living in Canada wants to send an invitation to the Russians to invade Victoria and Vancouver. 'The two cities would be the ideal entry point for an occupying force headed into the North American heartland,' he says. Hoping that Canada would become the grainbowl of the world after a nuclear clash between the superpowers, he reckons that 'the only good defence against atomic war is not to be hit'. (*Canadian Times Colonist*)

New Yorkers who move to more peaceful settings, but find themselves missing the general racket, can now buy a cassette of New York street noises. It's being sold by a New York firm with the appropriate name Twisted Minds Ltd. (*Wall St Journal*)

A Norwich hotel owner has offered a special weekend package for bureaucrats, for England's long Bank Holiday weekend. Bureaucrat guests will feel right at home when they check into the Hotel Nelson, owned by Peter Mackness. First, there will be a visitors' book to sign in triplicate. Then they will cut a red tape to get into their rooms, where they will find a welcoming memorandum. The £75 weekend package will include two-hour lunches, part of that time will be needed just to read the menu – six pages of small print written in obscure jargon. Tea is to be served hourly. Mackness says his plan was born out of his own frustrating experiences at local government offices. (*The Times*)

If you're continually finding yourself trapped in boring conversations that seem to go on forever, Hallad Paging Systems of Los Angeles has come up with a device to rescue you – a fake beeper. The device, which sells for $29.95, will start beeping, summoning you to an important phone call, moments after you secretly press a button. Hallad can be reached by writing to 6546 Hollywood Blvd, Suite 201, LA 90028. Sorry, but according to the information operator, they don't appear to have a phone – not a real one, anyway. (Los Angeles Times)

Vampire bats have their own taste preferences, say researchers at the Denver Wildlife Research Centre. When given a choice, they tend to avoid blood that's salty, sour or bitter tasting. But they're not finicky – they'll drink whatever blood's available, which means you can spike their blood with poisons and they'll still lap it up. (*Science & Mechanics*)

You can now study the Bible on a computer screen. Bible Research Systems of Austin, Texas has recorded the entire Bible on a computer program called 'The *Word* Processor'. It makes Bible study so easy, it's a miracle. Simply punch in a particular word, and the computer will quote every biblical passage where that word appears. (*Christian Science Monitor*)

The common practice of giving patients suffering from chronic pain drugs to reduce their anxiety only makes the pain worse, according to a study conducted by National Institute of Mental Health psychiatrist Thomas W. Uhde. He found that high anxiety increases the brain's production of its own painkiller noradrenaline, and that anxious patients therefore feel less pain. (Science News)

If you're visiting someone in the hospital, forget the flowers and bring food instead, advises *American Health* magazine. A University of Alabama Medical Centre study found that up to half of all patients in hospital for more than two weeks become malnourished, and this increases their chances of dying. One problem is that sick people lose their appetites, but that's understandable when confronted with hospital food. (*Moneysworth*)

The *Washington Post*'s 'Ear' column reports that the newest home-design rage among New York's trendy set is bathrooms without doors. You can see the toilets and their chic users in a feature spread in the June issue of *House and Garden* magazine. (*Washington Post*, 'Ear')

90

Japanese animal lovers are howling about a new bark-stopping dog collar that's started appearing on the streets. Every time the dog opens its yap to bark, its expanded vocal chords touch an electric terminal and it receives a jolt. The idea is that after a while the dog knows better than to even try barking. (Sunday Times)

The letter carrier approaches the house and finds a fierce-looking Doberman, growling his head off on the unfenced front lawn. But the postal employee proceeds to deliver the mail, knowing that an invisible fence separates them. That's the kind of situation John Purtell envisages for his product. Purtell is head of the Sta-Put Invisible Fence Co., based in New York, which is offering home-owners who don't like walls and fences another way to keep their pets fenced in. The invisible fence is a thin copper-coated wire embedded 4 to 6 inches underground around the edge of the property. A transmitter in the house sends a radio signal to the wire, and the dog wears a collar equipped with a tiny receiver. When the animal wanders within 5 feet of the wire, it gets a warning beep. If it ignores that and comes closer, it receives a mild electric shock sufficient to stop further wanderings. Purtell says the SPCA has already given its approval. It's been marketed in a few cities so far – 800 were sold last year in Philadelphia, with only a handful taking advantage of a money-back guarantee. Use with horses and cattle is also foreseen, thus bringing back the wide open spaces. (Knight-Rider News Service, *Chicago Tribune*)

The use of candlelight to create a romantic mood has a sound basis in biochemistry, says behavioral specialist Sean Thorton. According to *Into* magazine, Thorton explains that burning candles give off negative ions which, when breathed, make a person 'alert, energetic and very much in the mood for love'. (*Intro Magazine*)

Seiko, Japan's largest watch-maker, has announced the production of the world's first wristwatch with a built-in TV screen. The unit not only gets VHF, UHF, and FM radio – it comes with earphones – but it also features a digital display that tells you the time. (Palm Springs Desert Sun)

You've probably been wondering when this would come along – Riverton, Connecticut solar contractor Joel Gordes had designed a solar bomb shelter, simply by adding a sun room to the typical lead-encased shelter. He guarantees a refund if purchasers are not satisfied within twenty-one days of a nuclear attack. (*Energy News*)

A moving company in Mendocino, California goes by the name 'The Hernia Hauling Company'. Its motto is 'U Can Truss Us'. (Herb Caen, *San Francisco Chronicle*)

Love can hurt, says a study reported in *Doctor* magazine. Or it can itch. A survey of 227 American college students found that young people falling in love for the first time experienced a particularly high incidence of headaches, colds and skin rashes during the first six months of the affair. Breaking up was also hard on the system, but that's to be expected. (*Sunday Express*)

For those who like to get every last bit of goodness out of their cigarette, a North Miami, Florida inventor has patented a chewable cigarette filter. Sam F. Patarra's invention is a cigarette mouthpiece with removable back-to-back filters which flavour the smoke. The filter closest to the mouth can be chewed like gum. (Venture Magazine)

British Government scientists at the Meat Research Institute in Bristol have developed a chemical test that could prove very useful to lovers of fast-food hamburgers. The simple test involves applying to the hamburger a substance containing antibodies able to recognise the individual chemical 'fingerprints' of different kinds of meat. The antibodies will turn a bit of hamburger meat different colours, depending on whether it's, say, from a cow, a horse, a kangaroo, or whatever. (*Daily Telegraph*)

A Hong Kong inventor has applied for a patent for a stiff new alcoholic drink which he says is 'a carefully balanced health tonic'. In case you haven't guessed, it's 'antler brandy', containing deer antlers, sea horse, turtle shell, aloeswood and many other exotic ingredients. They are mixed with French brandy, allowed to stand for three months, then filtered. (*Chicago Tribune*)

Here's a new bit of information that wine snobs can use. Next time a dinner companion comments on a wine's corky, musty taste, simply inform them: 'That's the 2, 4, 6-trichloroanisole.' Researcher Hans-Rudolf Buser and colleagues at the Swiss Federal Research Station in Wadenswil, Switzerland, have identified 2, 4, 6-trichloroanisole as the chemical that leaks into wine from corks. (Science News)

Count Dracula would have been a more pleasant sort of chap if he had had the benefits of modern medicines to control his allergy to blood, says Dr Thomas McDevitt, an Idaho physician. McDevitt says that Count Dracula was a pain to be around, being 'utterly miserable' and 'savage', because he suffered from both an addiction to blood and an allergy to blood. (*Los Angeles Daily News*)

There seems to be a reason for pretty well everything in nature, and that includes big noses, say anthropologists James W. Carey and A. T. Steegman Jr. They say a big nose means your ancestors lived in a very dry or very cold climate. They determined this by nosing around into the snout sizes of people of various races and locations. The nose functions as a humidifier and heater of air, and people in cold or dry climates just need a bigger heating–humidifying unit. (*The Guardian*)

The designer diaper is here. General Diaper Service of St Louis is supplying its customers with special dress-up diapers, meant for special occasions, that bear the logo of the cotton industry, with one difference. General Diaper's General Manager, Cal Miner, says: 'The cotton industry uses a brown logo. We couldn't – for obvious reasons.' It's part of a campaign to promote the cotton diaper over the throwaway sort. (St Louis Post-Dispatch)

A new device being introduced jointly by United Technologies Corp. and Tishman Realty and Construction Co. of New York could wind up saving the Federal Government piles of money on its electricity bill. The 'Infracon' will switch office lights off automatically twelve minutes after all motion ceases in the office, as indicated by sensors on the ceiling. Since the sensors can pick up even minimal movement, in effect the lights will go off after someone leaves the office or falls asleep at his desk. It will also switch on the lights when someone enters, or awakens. (*Wall St Journal*)

The most effective locker-room pep talks aren't fiery orations meant to arouse athletes to a frenzy. In fact, they're delivered so softly, they tend to put athletes asleep. That's according to Dr Peter Weston, Chairman of the Meadow Bank Sports Medical Centre in Glasgow. He says that some top athletes are already successfully using hypnosis to improve their performance, by controlling anxiety. That's especially true of Eastern European nations, whose teams regularly travel with professional hypnotherapists. (*Daily Telegraph*)

Two researchers at the Otago Medical School in Auckland, New Zealand have proposed that warning labels be put on packages of liquorice candy. Dr F. O. Simpson and I. J. Currie checked out 603 high school students and concluded that liquorice is 'semi-addictive'. One-fifth of the students reported cravings for liquorice that could lead to consumption in dosages high enough to cause muscle pains, headaches, nausea, high blood pressure and lowered potassium levels. (Popular Science)

People who'd rather ward off heathens than worry about space invaders are in luck. A Toronto non-profit organisation has developed a selection of Christian video games. Frank Venezia, founder of Christian Computer-based Communications says: 'We're trying to show programmers that they can develop games with Christian values rather than just shoot-em-up themes.' (*Ottawa Citizen*)

A growing number of imaginative computer programmers are booby-trapping the programs they sell to companies, *Business Week* magazine reports. If the customer doesn't pay money owed for the program within a specified time period, the program is rigged to shut off and gum up the works. (*Chicago Tribune*)

Cattle prefer Playboy *magazine to the* Christian Science Monitor *by a wide margin, with the* Washington Post *somewhere in the middle,* Playboy *reports. The cattle find* Playboy *more digestible, according to experiments conducted for the US Agriculture Department by Dr Peter van Soest of Cornell University. The experiments involved adding finely ground newspapers and magazines to beef-cattle feed. The paper is a good source of carbohydrates.* (Playboy)

What are parents to do if they find their son playing with dolls? Let him play, says Dr Henri Parens, a psychiatrist at the Medical College of Pennsylvania. He says the nurturing behaviour the boy is displaying with his dolls may well make him a better father later on. (*Family Weekly*)

Handwriting seems to reflect personality in the case of persons suffering from anorexia nervosa, the psychiatric disorder characterised by out-of-control fasting. According to psychiatric studies at Oxford University, the handwriting of anorexics is frequently extremely small – so tiny, in fact, that often a magnifying glass is required to read it. (*Family Weekly*)

In many homes these days, television serves as 'little more than a talking lamp', says Elizabeth J. Roberts, President of Television Audience Assessment Inc., which surveyed 1,580 viewers in Springfield, Illinois. Three-quarters of the people who weren't watching alone were talking to someone else while the TV jabbered on. Twenty per cent were doing household chores; 17 per cent were reading; 6 per cent were talking on the phone, and 12 per cent were engaged in other leisure pursuits. (*Wall St Journal*)

Just as humans are becoming increasingly disgruntled with so-called 'plastic' food, Kansas State University animal nutritionist Ernie Bartley has come up with a plastic hay substitute for cattle. He says the plastic hay is cheaper, half of it can be recovered for reuse from manure, and it cleans out the intestines like real hay. Also, it spares humans and cattle alike the runny noses and eyes due to allergies to hay. (Omni Magazine)

Dairy farmers will be happy to hear that researchers have come across a nomadic East African tribe, the Masai, that lives almost solely on milk, and they are healthier than neighbouring farming tribes that consume more of a balanced diet, according to University of Minnesota Cardiology Professor Dr John Murray, who presented his findings to the annual meeting of the American Heart Association in Dallas. The Masai are virtually immune to the rheumatic fever and accompanying heart disease that plague that region of the world, and Murray attributes that to high levels of oleic acid in their milk. He says, 'It's a good choice for them because they live in an area of mostly desert scrubs.' The Masai are 'very cattle oriented', says Murray. They spend their leisure time sitting around swapping cattle stories and singing cattle songs, and live in houses made of cattle dung, perhaps the ultimate tribute to their cows. However, Murray doesn't advise Westerners to try to copy them. (*Chicago Tribune*)

Residents near Hudson, Colorado who have been burned up over their flammable water now at least have an explanation from State officials. Folks in Weld County have been able, of late, to light their drinking water with a match and keep the flame going for several minutes. According to John Rold, director of the Colorado Geological Survey, a likely cause is methane gas entering the water supply from underground rock formations. (*Los Angeles Times*)

A drug that could be the lazy person's way to burn off fat is being developed by at least three American drug companies, the *Washington Post* reports. The drug would burn off fat without the need to exercise, by imitating the metabolic effects of exercise. Lilly Research Laboratories seem to have taken this work the farthest. So far, tests on rats, mice and beagles have been encouraging, but it is estimated that it would be another five fat years before such a drug was available to the public. (*Washington Post*)

A nagging wife can help a man live to a ripe old age, says Dr Robert Butler, Director of the US National Institute on Ageing. He says women don't nag their husbands enough. In his own words, 'They can probably nag them a little more on certain things — to be moderate in smoking and drinking, for instance, and keeping them physically more active.' (*Reuters*, Toronto Globe & Mail)

They can have sex but they never fall in love. These are people who have had their pituitary gland removed, according to Dr John Money, a medical psychologist at Johns Hopkins Medical School in Baltimore, who's just completed a fifteen-year study of such unfortunates. Though they may have an active sex life, says Money, they remain 'romantically inert', because pituitary surgery disturbs the hypothalamic nerve passageways which transmit love messages, as well as other emotions. (*Chicago Tribune*)

Many people are harmed because they don't get enough stress in their lives, says *Executive Fitness Newsletter* researcher Milton Holmen. He says that people suffering from insufficient stress may find it hard to get out of bed in the morning, and may get involved in activities to raise their stress level that wind up getting them into trouble. University of Pennyslvania researchers found, by administering shocks to rats and giving some rats the ability to control their shocks, that rats who could control their stress levels did a better job fighting off cancer tumours than rats who had no control, and also were more successful in fighting cancer than rats who had no stress at all. (*Chicago Tribune*)

They laughed at Ronald Reagan when he said that trees cause air pollution. But now the Environmental Protection Agency says it has a study in its hands that backs the

President up – to a point. According to the study, performed by Environmental Research & Technology Inc. trees emit hydrocarbons that form ozone, a prime ingredient in smog. But, before you get out your axe, the study notes that tree-made pollutants must mix with man-made pollutants for this to happen, and that also, in the words of project director Fred Lurmann, trees play 'a key role in purifying the air', as 'scavengers' of ozone. (Washington Post)

The US Patent Office has awarded a patent for a revolutionary new condom that bursts open during intercourse. Actually, just a compartment in the condom bursts, releasing anti-VD medication. Another newly patented device is a toothbrush with a handle that dispenses toothpaste into the bristles. (*Chicago Tribune*)

Scientific investigators have come across a species of bee in Brazil that is not only resistant to DDT but actually gathers the pesticide, as a sort of hobby. Dr Donald Roberts, then of the University of Brazil, was studying malaria-transmitting mosquitos when he found bees along the Ituxi river with high concentrations of DDT used to spray mosquitos. And wooden boards sprayed with DDT attracted large numbers of the bees, males of the species *Euphuesia Purpurata*. Dr Roberts writes in *Nature* magazine that the bees' love of DDT became a real nuisance for local residents, because the bees would swarm into houses to collect the DDT that accumulated on inside walls. They didn't sting, but the constant buzzing was irritating. Dr Roberts thinks the bees may be mistaking the pesticide for one of their natural attractants. They flew off with so much DDT, he says, that they hurt the spraying effort. (*Nature*)

Funny TV commercials work well for cat food but not for dog food, according to the ad-testing firm McCollum, Spielman & Co. of Great Neck, New York which analysed TV commercials to determine how memorable and persuasive they were. A spokesman for the firm says that humour works for cats but not dogs, because 'dogs just aren't as funny as cats'. (Wall Street Journal)

Doctors writing in the *New England Journal of Medicine* have issued another warning about the dangers of a diet. This time, it involved a Canadian woman who ate a Kleenex box and a cigarette package almost daily for twelve years. She came down with mercury poisoning. (*Wall Street Journal*)

A dentist identified only as a 'Dr R.H.' has developed an outline for a proposed communications device for use by dental patients whose mouths are otherwise occupied. The device, according to *Advertising Age's* 'Idea Market-Place' section, could be held by the patient or attached to the chair arm. Pushing the appropriate buttons would light up a screen with phrases like: 'Yes', 'No', 'Need to rinse', 'Need to swallow', 'Ouch' and 'Stop please'. Dentists may well prefer the expense of this device to the pain of a bitten finger. (*Advertising Age*)

Researchers at the International Development Research Centre have come up with a building material for houses that is cheap, remarkably durable, easy to use, and cools better in summer and warms better in winter than other materials in use. That material is mud. Some mud homes 1,000 years old are still in use in the Middle East, the Centre reports. And research indicates that the mud can be further improved by mixing in asphalt or boiled banana stems. (*Toronto Globe & Mail*)

Panhandlers will do better if they dress up when working airports. On the other hand, if they want to work a bus station, they'll make more money wearing grubbier clothes. That's the conclusion of a study by Wayne E. Hensley of the Dept of Communication Studies at Virginia Polytechnic in Blacksburg. He had students, dressed well and poorly, ask travellers for dimes for phone calls. His conclusion was that people help their own kind. (Psychology Today)

A Geneva, Switzerland company, Consortrad, is marketing a precise miniature compass that assures Moslems around the world that they are facing Mecca when they pray. According to the company, some devout Moslems have expressed concern that, without accurate guidance, their prayers may be erroneously directed to Tel Aviv. The plain model of the 'Mecca Module' costs $750, with more elaborate platinum and jewel-studded models selling for up to a hundred times that. (*San Francisco Chronicle*)

CCS Communication Control of New York is now offering Do-It-Yourself Car Bulletproofing Kits. They include windows. Prices are in the $20,000–$30,000 range – a small price to pay for peace of mind out on the road. (*Playboy*)

There's some consolation in losing, say researchers Klaus Miczek, Michael Thompson and Louis Schuster of Tufts University. The losers get doses of opiates to dull the pain of defeat, compliments of the body's own anti-pain centres. That was the case with mice who were put into the cages of other mice who attack – and drove them off. Tests on the defeated mice showed up the presence of morphine-like anti-pain substances. And that may well be the case with humans too. (*New York Times*)

It will be easy for children to make believe they're driving the real thing, if they have a toy car, from Paragon-Reiss of New York, that was recently introduced at a Dallas Toy Show. The $7,000, 6-feet-long plaything comes complete with a five horsepower engine capable of attaining a top speed of 20 mph, an electronic ignition system, automatic transmission, lights, radio and wide sport wheels. And it's easy on gas; it gets an estimated 60 miles to the gallon. (Los Angeles Daily News)

Lorin F. Sowards of Brownville, Nebraska has patented a doorbell for pets. It rings when the animal pushes plates mounted on the inside and outside of a door. (*New York Times*)

People who are subjected to loud rock 'n' roll, and don't like rock music, will be even more annoyed to hear this news: according to David Lipscomb, Director of the University of Tennessee's Noise Research Laboratory, loud music causes more hearing damage to people who dislike the music, than to those who are 'grooving' on it. He explains that the stress caused by high-volume noise results in a constriction of blood vessels, so that the ear gets less oxygen and nutrients when it needs them more. But people enjoying the music experience less stress. Which is why, he suspects, the rock musicians he's seen exhibit less hearing impairment than would have been expected. (*Science News*)

At last, there's a suggestion for combating cigarette smoking that smokers will love. Dr Albert Castro, of the University of Miami Medical School, says – put more nicotine in each cigarette. Nicotine is what smokers crave, and also, says Castro – and other medical experts agree – nicotine is less harmful than other harmful tobacco ingredients. (*Atlanta Journal*)

If you find yourself being closely circled by bats, don't panic – it's your lucky break, says Marty Fujita, a Boston University doctoral student who's a bat expert. She says the bats are after the bugs and mosquitos around you. And they're interested in 'checking you out', purely out of curiosity. (Vancouver Sun)

There's no longer any need to come out of your backyard swimming pool to take a phone call. You don't even have to float to the surface, thanks to an underwater telephone being sold by Hammacher Schlemmer of New York. If you want one, you'll be soaked for $795. And, if your motorised lawn mower doesn't make cutting the grass easy enough, the firm is also selling a lawn mower without wheels. It floats on an air cushion. (*Advertising Age*)

Having no legs is a handicap on earth, but is actually an advantage in the zero-gravity environment of space, says occupational therapist Trisha Thompson, of the Hastings College of Law in San Francisco. She is working on a joint Hastings/NASA research project exploring the use of amputees on space missions. Thompson says that doctors with the skylab space station programme of the early 1970s found that legs were a handicap in zero-gravity conditions. They get bruised while floating through hatchways, and require food, oxygen and time-consuming exercise (*Omni Magazine*)

Unsafe at any velocity – that's the US Army's verdict on 30 million rounds of ammunition being stored at the Rocky Mountain arsenal in Denver. The Army wants to destroy the bullets, fearing they are a health hazard because of DDT contamination. The pesticide was sprayed on the bullets in Vietnam, to prevent Vietnamese bugs from sneaking into the US on them. (Portland Oregonian)

103

The Mayor of Beirut, Mitri Naamar, is a supreme civic optimist. He says that the present devastation will make it all the easier to proceed with his plans for urban redevelment, which involve reconstructing the downtown core and decentralising commercial activities. These plans date back from 1975. At that time, the city would have had to pay a huge wreckers' bill. The Mayor also plans to build a subway system, which now won't require as much digging as it would have before. (*Christian Science Monitor*)

The US Bureau of Printing and Engraving is scouting around for a town that's just the right size – too small for the Russians to bother nuking, but large enough to supply 100 to 200 workers for a new plant. The Bureau needs to build a back-up printing plant in just such a place, so that it can continue turning out stamps and paper currency after the nuclear bombs strike. Project Co-ordinator Ken Farrow says: 'We're looking for something that's not listed as a high-risk area.' He has a list of fifty possible sites right now. The plant would handle about 18 per cent of the Bureau's printing load in the interim period before a nuclear war. (*Washington Post*)

Wait – don't throw away that leftover food. Smear it on your face instead. That's the message from Riquette Hofstein, who's been promoting the beauty-enhancing advantages of table scraps the world over, and has now established a clinic in Hollywood, California. For example, she says, mashed overripe bananas or avocados are excellent lighteners of age spot or freckles. Grated raw potato placed in gauze on your eyes gets rid of those circles underneath. Mashed kitty litter mixed with water is a good facial mask for oily skin. For best results, unused kitty litter is recommended. Raw egg whites make a good facial mask, and the yolks can be used as moisturiser. *Jelly is a good setting lotion for hair. And if a child gets chewing gum stuck in his hair, she suggests simply lathering peanut butter into the hair, and the gum will comb out.* (Los Angeles Times)

Welfare Cadillac

34-YEAR-OLD Irma Mae Smith of Alexandria, Louisiana has been sentenced to five years in prison for welfare fraud. She was rather blatant about it. The licence plates on her luxury car read 'Welfare Cadillac'. (*Washington Post*)

Lady Luck didn't smile on Ihab Abbas. The 20-year-old Egyptian, an illegal immigrant to England, stole a friend's birth certificate so that he could get a driver's licence and a British passport. But he ran into trouble when he used the ID to apply for a job, in his friend's name, with the London Metropolitan Police. As luck would have it, while his application was being processed, the friend was charged with murdering a 66-year-old woman by kicking and jumping on her. Abbas was fined £350 and held for deportation. (*Daily Telegraph*)

A burglar who broke into the Pittsford, Michigan home of David A. Simons stole only one item – the burglar alarm, worth $100. (San Diego Union)

A teenager in Kuwait who was sentenced to six months in prison for kissing his fiancée on a public beach appealed against the sentence on the grounds that they were ready to get married. Kuwait's Court of Appeal agreed that the sentence was in error – it sentenced the youth to forty-two months in prison. The fact that the girl was only 15 weighed heavily on the court. (*Daily Telegraph*)

Birmingham, Alabama City Council has decided that it would be unreasonable to require go-go dancers to carry an identification card 'on their persons' at all times. (*Houston Chronicle*)

Police in North Pownal, New York arrested a Hoosick Falls man after finding him asleep in a stolen vehicle. Charged was one Ralph Wideawake. (Nat'l Lampoon)

The FBI blew an investigation of case-fixing in Cleveland Municipal Court by paying thousands of dollars in bribe money to impostors who posed as judges, the *Cleveland Plain Dealer* reports. The problem, said the paper, was that the FBI never bothered to find out what its bribe targets looked like. One 34-year-old man successfully posed as a 68-year-old judge. The investigation produced only one arrest – for embezzlement and tax evasion. (*San Francisco Chronicle*)

Sri Lanka has banned the capture of wild elephants, which was depleting the stock. The new law has brought complaints from people who need a steady supply of elephants in their enterprises. These include Buddhist temples, festival promoters and the logging industry. (*National Review*)

A 32-year-old man is legally entitled to adopt his 43-year-old homosexual lover as a son, the New York State Supreme Court has ruled. In reversing a Manhattan family court decision, Justice Sidney Asch wrote: 'At first blush, it may seem a perversion of the adoption process ... however, the best description of a family is a continuing relationship of love and care and an assumption of responsibility for some other person.' (San Francisco Chronicle)

Nicaragua's Government censor, who reviews the proofs of all newspaper pages before they can be published, recently banned a photograph of an elephant on water skis. The censor, 23-year-old Nelba Blandon, explained that viewing an elephant on skis might have distracted people from the urgent tasks of the revolution. She said: 'There is freedom of expression here but there is no freedom of expression for the counter-revolution.' (*Chicago Tribune*)

Britain's Department of Transport has announced that after 1 October it will issue no new licences for trolley bus drivers. The official reason given is that there are no trolley buses left in service. (*The Times*)

A new ordinance passed by the South Sharleston, W. Virginia City Council brings no legislative relief for the city's cats. It is now against the law for a cat to relieve itself on property other than its owner's. (Sacramento Bee)

Woodbridge, New Jersey hairdresser Richard Anzovino says he'll appeal against the $50 disorderly conduct fine he received for sealing customer Susan Salvatore's hairdo with a kiss. Anzovino admits he told her to close her eyes, but he contends then simply placed two fingers over her lips and made a kissing sound. (*Denver Post*)

A 19-year-old Welsh railway signalman has admitted to half a dozen instances in which he placed concrete blocks across the tracks in the path of oncoming passenger trains. Paul David Wescombe told Cardiff Crown Court that he did it to relieve job boredom. He was ordered to be detained for psychiatric reports. (*Daily Telegraph*)

The Superior Court of Pennsylvania has declared valid the common law marriage last year of a 36-year-old teacher and a 14-year-old girl who was an eighth-grade student of his. The court pointed out that under state law a male and female can become man and wife by declaring their desire to marry in front of witnesses, as long as they are at least 7 years old. Edward Christoph lost his teaching job in Erie because of his marriage, but the court ruling will probably save him from prosecution, as well as gain him back his wife, who was sent off to California by a juvenile court order. (Miami Herald)

A Cedar Rapids, Iowa grocery clerk who was fired after a supervisor heard him loudly belch in the presence of a customer was unjustly dismissed, a State hearing officer has ruled. Therefore, Wayne Ditsworth is entitled to collect unemployment compensation, said the officer, Steven Beasley. He ruled that expelling 'gas or wind spasmodically from the stomach through the mouth is usually not wilful or deliberate behaviour'. Ditsworth said he didn't realise the customer was around. (*San Franciso Chronicle*)

The California Senate elections committee has approved a bill that would require political candidates mailing campaign material within fifteen days of an election to place on the material a warning that some of the statements contained therein might not be true. The required statement would say: '*Warning*: be on guard for campaign literature distributed in the final days before an election. It can contain distortions and misrepresentations of the truth without affording an opportunity for opponents to respond.' (*Los Angeles Daily News*)

Hallmark Cards is offering a new line of 'Lite' greeting cards, advertised as a 'third less serious than regular greeting cards'. (*Wall Street Journal*)

Thieves who stole three crossbows from a Hoddesdon, Hertfordshire shop could be in for a sharp disappointment, warns the shopowner, Terry Goulden. He says one of the bows was rigged to shoot backwards. It was made for use in a film. (Sunday Express)

Just how desperate a plight toothache can be was demonstrated by a 33-year-old Chicago man, who perched himself on a third-floor ledge at Chicago's Cook County Hospital and threatened to jump unless he was given medicine for his toothache. He was taken away for observation of his head. (*Jet Magazine*)

When the new City Council was elected last month, Pagedale, Missouri Mayor Mary Hall predicted smooth sailing from then on in the town of 4,500 known for its political squabbling. But things have only got worse. The town now has three police chiefs on the payroll. Aldermen handed Chief Merlin Guyor his walking papers, but he continues to draw his pay and man his office. The aldermen hired Odis Williams to be chief, but then the Mayor hired Moses King as chief. Chief Williams then arrested Chief King for speeding and disturbing the peace. Chief King said he couldn't be arrested because he was chief. Chief Williams then arrested Mayor Hall for disturbing the peace which is a charge that perhaps should be laid against the whole lot of them. (*San Diego Union*)

Ronald W. Mays, the Franktown, Colorado artist who broke into the Denver Art Museum last November to hang one of his paintings, will have his wish fulfilled, as part of his sentence. Denver District Judge Raymond Jones, a veritable hanging judge, has ordered Mays to donate one of his works to the Mayor's Commission on the Arts, for display at a location of the Commission's

110

choosing. The judge says he wouldn't be surprised if the Commission selected his own chamber. Mays indicated to the judge that he'd donate the same painting he tried to donate to the Museum. He was also sentenced to sixty-five days in jail, which was time already served. (Denver Post)

According to statistics released by San Diego Police, nine out of every ten applicants rated as qualified to be San Diego police officers admit to having used marijuana or other drugs. Eighty-seven per cent of the police applicants say they've smoked grass, and 31.8 per cent admit to using cocaine. The police require recruits to be grass-free for six months, and cocaine-free for a year. (*San Diego Union*)

When panicky drug smugglers, surprised by the coastguard, clear their boats off the Florida Keys by tossing hundreds of bales of marijuana overboard, the waters don't stay littered for long. Young and old residents of the Keys – housewives, business people, teens and grandparents alike, wade into the water and pitch in to clean up the green flotsam. Coastguard officials aren't sure how the citizens dispose of the marijuana litter but, at $5,000 to $10,000 per dried bale, it is suspected that folks are indeed cleaning up. (*Detroit Free Press*)

The FBI has the same problem many other renters face – some of its favourite stake-out apartments are being converted into condominiums, says FBI director, William Webster. Rather than see agents tossed out on to the sidewalk with their binoculars and bugging equipment, he's asking Congress for some money to buy the condos. (US News & World Reporter)

In the last few months, undercover drug operations in Georgia by State and Federal agents have led to the arrests, on drug-smuggling and trafficking charges, of six different county sheriffs and ex-sheriffs, 6 deputy sheriffs, 2 police chiefs, 2 county commissioners, 2 state troopers, 9 police officers, a police narcotics agent, a state investigator, a prison warden, 2 deputy prison wardens, and 8 coastguard sailors. Also arrested was a Georgia state senator who wanted drug smugglers to finance his campaign for governor. A crackdown in Florida has led smugglers to look further up the coast, and a lot of backwoods-type officials have never seen that kind of money being flashed around before. (*Washington Post*)

A 25-year-old Jamaican immigrant told a Calgary, Alberta court that he robbed a bank as a result of advice from Canadian immigration officials. Oliver Nelson said that he was starving and sleeping in parks, and decided to ask immigration officials to ship him back to Jamaica. He said they told him they could only do that if he committed a crime. It appears he'll get his wish, eventually. (*Portland Oregonian*)

Rarely in the annals of crime has so yellow a crime been committed. John Maloney returned to his South London semi-detached home from a vacation to discover that burglars had painted the entire inside of the home yellow. A Scotland Yard spokesman said the paint job, which included all the furniture, must have taken 'quite some time'. He said, 'It really is quite an amazing sight. Every part of the house is covered.' The painters also made off with £4,000 worth of property. (*Daily Telegraph*)

In Newark, New Jersey, embezzlement charges were filed against a prison inmate who charged his long-distance phone calls without authorisation to another number – a number belonging to the FBI. 25-year-old Joseph Pomp Booker made frequent phone calls to his family in Alabama, and tried to stick the feds with the bill. (St Louis Post-Dispatch)

A Mastic, New York woman who phoned her Jewish neighbour, with whom she had been quarrelling, on the Jewish New Year, Rosh Hashana, to wish her a 'Happy Jew Day' has become the first person to be convicted under a new New York State law that prohibits harassment with racial or ethnic slurs. Jeanette Poggioni could have received up to a year in prison, but a judge in Hauppage, NY instead assigned her thirty-five hours of community work. The 25-year-old housewife said she had nothing against Jews, but just didn't like Marsha Falik, her neighbour. They had argued over their kids. (*Miami Herald*)

Accused bank robber David Kloster hit a bank in Lafayette, Louisiana, then laundered his illicit money at a laundrette, according to a person who was held as a hostage by Kloster for several hours. The hostage said that the 23-year-old robber stopped at a laundrette to wash and dry the money, which had been stained red by booby-trapped dyes. He was arrested in Vinton, Los Angeles (*Sacramento Bee*)

A preliminary hearing on a burglary charge against 20-year-old James Moore of Westminster, Colorado was cancelled by an Adams County Judge after burglary victim Earl Horn noticed that the defendant was wearing his stolen jacket. Moore was ordered to stand trial. (Denver Post)

Police held a clothes line-up at Bicester Police Station. People were invited to come by and try to select their own belongings from among more than 300 items of under-wear, nighties, skirts and dresses that had been pinched from local clothes lines as they hung drying. Police discovered the clothes at the home of a 34-year-old man. (*Daily Telegraph*)

Burglars broke into Eastchurch Prison on the Isle of Sheppey and made off with a television and video unit valued at £600. According to police, it wasn't an inside job. (*Daily Telegraph*)

Traffic Court Judge Loren J. Kabbes, who handles all drunken driving cases in Coles County, Illinois, is to appear in court in Mattoon on 1 June on a drunk driving charge. The judge had refused to take a breathaliser test when police approached him as he pulled into his driveway. (New Orleans Times-Picayune)

A British High Court cleared Leeds pub owner Dennis Markham of charges that he shortchanged customers by serving up pints of beer with a half-inch head, instead of full pints of liquid. He was charged after an inspector received a pint glass with a good head on top. High Court Justice Webster noted: 'In the Leeds area, customers demand a beer with a tight creamy head, served within the glass so that it does not disappear but follows the liquid down the inside of the glass as the liquid is drunk.' He said that if the inspector didn't want a head, he should have said so. (*Daily Telegraph*)

When police in Madras, India arrested 25-year-old Venka Tesan for burglary, he told them where half the loot could be found – in the vaults of the Temple of the Goddess Amman, at Mangadu. And police found that to be the case. Tesan explained: 'I was brought up to believe in donating part of my income to the Temple. And I am still a very religious man.' (*Sunday Express*)

A man apparently upset over being denied unemployment benefits walked into a Kansas Division of Employment office in Kansas City and assaulted a computer; according to the office manager, Ed Berridge, the man picked up a computer terminal and dropped it on the floor. The computer was apparently an innocent victim. Said Berridge: 'There was no provocation.' The assailant was arrested and jailed a short time later. (Palm Springs Desert Sun)

Anthony Fairchild was the star of his own television series in his Denver neighbourhood, but he didn't like it a bit. However, the US District Court has now dismissed his invasion of privacy suit against the drug enforcement administration. DEA agents, who suspected Fairchild of manufacturing cocaine, mounted a TV camera on a power pole outside Fairchild's house, and trained it on the home. But Fairchild's doings attained wider fame, because the TV signal was picked up by neighbours' TV sets. (*Denver Post*)

For an all-night dispatcher at police headquarters in Arroyo Grande, California a visit by an irate citizen was like something out of a late-night TV movie. The man entered the station wearing Indian warpaint and a mohawk haircut, waving a razor and screaming war chants. San Luis Obispo County Sheriff's deputies were summoned, and arrived just as the man was leaping the counter. William Ommny was booked for investigation of threatening public services and possessing a deadly weapon – the razor blade. (*Sacramento Bee*)

Police in Hastings, Michigan said they wouldn't file criminal charges against 70-year-old Jack Wilson and 65-year-old Gertrude Cremer, who strolled out of their senior citizens' home, stole a car, and went on a 50-mile joyride. Said Police Chief Mark Steinfort: 'I think they just got together and decided to go for a ride. There was no criminal intent.' (Chicago Tribune)

A young man who broke out of jail in Mason, Michigan, was recaptured after he lay down on a front lawn to read a newspaper. Sadly, for 18-year-old Ralph Bosse, the lawn belonged to a sheriff's deputy. (*Chicago Tribune*)

Fear of crime led Leonie Haddad, a 66-year-old widow, to decide that she no longer wanted to live alone in her Santa Monica, California home. So she contacted a non-profit roommate–housemate referral service, Senior Housing Assistance in Sharing. They hooked her up with 60-year-old Betty Mae Page. But Haddad began to have doubts about her new housemate, particularly on the morning last July when she awoke to find Page lying on top of her, brandishing a knife, and screaming, 'God told me to kill you!' Her doubts increased as she was stabbed a dozen or so times before she was able to flee. She suffered a punctured lung and required plastic surgery on her face, hands and arms. It was only later that she learned, through Santa Monica police, that Page had been committed to a mental hospital in 1979 for allegedly stabbing a neighbour. She was released after less than a year. Now she's filed a $1.75 million lawsuit against the State of California, which operates the mental hospital, and the referral service, which was responsible for what, in hindsight, was a mismatch. (*Los Angeles Herald-Examiner*)

As drunk driving arrest records go, 42-year-old Mark Elvis Carroll may hold some kind of record. The Miami-area airline customer services agent was taken in for drunk driving four times in thirty-one hours. The first time, when he was found slumped behind the wheel of his station wagon, he was released on a $50 bond. Seven hours later, he was nabbed in similar circumstances, but walked out of the Dade County Jail by signing a 'promise to appear' form. That was how he also walked out after his third arrest. Because of shift changes, jailers didn't notice his repeat visits. A computer is supposed to keep track of that, but it's not equipped to handle return appearances so soon. Says Dade County Corrections Captain Kevin Hickey: 'It's usually a day or two behind.' Carroll finally dried out after his fourth arrest, when his car hopped a median and crashed into a van, sending the van's two occupants to hospital. This time, authorities got tough and required a $500 bond, which he couldn't meet. (*Miami Herald*)

Twenty-year-old Nancy McCabe told Des Moines, Iowa police that it was her lion cub who was at the wheel when her car drove into a downtown building. She said the lion got its paws tangled in the wheel. She was charged with drunk driving, but no charges were laid against the lion who, according to police investigator Tim Cunningham, 'appeared to be sober'. (St Louis Post-Dispatch)

Police had bad news, good news, and bad news for 20-year-old Chris Wallis of Paignton, Devon. The bad news was that his bicycle had been stolen while he slept. The good news was that the two culprits had been caught, and the bike recovered. The further bad news was that, while they were questioning the suspected thieves, the bicycle had been stolen again from outside the police station. But for Wallis, it was bad news enough just being woken up at four in the morning. He told police that if they had any more good news, 'Wait until a decent hour to come and tell me.' (*Daily Telegraph*)

Dade County, Florida Judge Alfred F. Nesbitt, who in 1979 dismissed eighty radar-related speeding cases on the grounds that radar-gun results are too unreliable to be used in court, is more convinced than ever of that now, after he was cited for speeding. A radar gun had him doing 63 mph, eight over the limit. Judge Nesbitt says: 'Now I know. It doesn't always work.' He says he had his cruise control set at 55. He'll fight the $25 fine. The judge put the brakes on radar-derived evidence in his court after TV newscasts showed trees clocked at 86 mph, and a house clocked at 20 mph. (*Miami Herald*)

In Columbus, Ohio, 61-year-old Richard J. Funk was charged with drunken driving and other offences after he struck about forty parked cars, one by one. (Portland Oregonian)

A New York State Supreme Court Justice has ordered an investigation of two misconduct charges against a New York criminal court judge whose informality has several times generated controversy. One charge relates to a widely publicised incident in which Judge Alan I. Friess tossed a coin to determine whether a convicted pickpocket received twenty days or thirty days in jail. Another charge is that, on his first week on the bench in 1979, Judge Friess asked courtroom spectators for a show of hands as to which of two men should be believed. The Judge has already been censured once, less than a year ago, for inviting a woman accused of murder, whom he had released, to spend the night at his home. The Judge had explained that she was low on money and had no place to stay. (*New York Times*)

118

Nobody guarded the four guardian angels that for sixty-six years stood watch outside the Most Holy Name of Jesus Church in St Louis. Nobody thought it was necessary, since the bronze statues each weighed 1,000 pounds, were embedded in concrete, and were of dubious artistic merit. In fact, a former pastor who wanted to get rid of them gave up because they were so heavy. But nothing is safe these days. The Rev. Norbert A. Mersinger speculated that the thieves required a crane and a truck. He thought they were taken for scrap value. (*St Louis Post-Dispatch*)

There's a moral in this story somewhere. Two thieves who stole cash from money boxes at an Atlantic, Iowa camping ground became so occupied with counting their loot that they crashed their getaway car. Rex Allen Bartelt and Donald Fredriksen, both 20 years old, were turned over to the authorities. (Chicago Tribune)

Two Bisonville, North Carolina teenagers who stole bubble gum from a 12-year-old boy have been ordered by a judge in Greensboro to repay the boy ten times the amount of bubble gum taken. Eight-year-old Willie Foust and 16-year-old Kenneth Simpson will have to come up with 60¢ worth of bubble gum for John Stallings, based on their original theft of 6¢ worth. Things could have been worse for the youths, though. Under the felony robbery charges they faced, they could have received up to ten years in prison. Guilford District Judge Edward Lowe also ordered the youths into a special counselling and community service programme. (*Los Angeles Times*)

A Cambridge, Massachusetts mathematician–physicist who hasn't mowed his lawn in fourteen years is entitled to let it keep on growing, a jury has ruled. Abdul Sayied was acquitted of a sanitary code violation, brought by the

City's Health Board after a neighbour, Frank Paone, complained. Sayied contended that 'grass is meant to grow'. (*Los Angeles Times*)

Medical reports from three different doctors have confirmed that former Ohio State Cashier Elizabeth Jane Boerger is genuinely disabled with amnesia. She can't even remember that she worked for the State, let alone what happened to $1.3 million in cash under her control that mysteriously vanished from the State Treasury, along with all pertinent records. The 48-year-old woman is now drawing a State Disability Pension for her amnesia. (New York Times)

An Iranian immigrant imprisoned for car theft has been convicted of using prison phones to obtain money fraudulently from a New York bank and from the International Monetary Fund, by posing as a Saudi Arabian Sheik. Ali Khouhestanian phoned Morgan Guaranty Bank President Robert Lindsay from a Massachusetts prison, and talked him into forwarding $43,500 to a female accomplice, supposedly for bail for the sheik's nephew, and for a house payment. Then, from a New York jail, he talked an International Monetary Fund official out of $25,000. The official thought he sounded pretty convincing. (*Sacramento Bee*)

Spreading the Lord's message had a crashing urgency for 38-year-old James Sanborn of Tampa, Florida. Sanborn says he was 'guided by the Lord' when he climbed into a cement mixer and smashed through the gates of the Marion Correctional Institution in Lowell, Florida, where he was an inmate. He only had a month to go before parole on his eight-month sentence for car theft and assault, but Sanborn says he was eager to get out to preach the Gospel, on instructions from God. He was captured a few minutes later when the cement truck ran off the road trying to dodge a road-block, and became bogged down in a field. Says the would-be-Holy-Roller: 'God saw fit to test me.' (*Miami Herald*)

District of Columbia police have filed robbery charges against John T. Crutchfield, who, they say, robbed a bank after escaping from a mental hospital, then returned to the hospital. Crutchfield had been committed to St Elizabeth's Hospital in Washington a year ago, after he was found not guilty, by reason of insanity, of robbing the same bank twice before. DC police say that, of the last twelve bank robberies in the District, at least four have been committed by escapees from St Elizabeth's Hospital, who had been placed there after being found innocent of bank robberies, due to insanity. The hospital is also home to John Hinckley Jr, by reason of insanity. (Washington Post)

Thieves who broke into a display case in a Rochester, New York shopping mall left $75,000 worth of antiques untouched, and made off with a pile of baseball cards. They were valued at more than $10,000. (*San Francisco Chronicle*)

I've had enough

A T the age of 91, Matilde Wirth has proved again that hell hath no fury like a woman scorned. She has filed for divorce, claiming her husband Rudolph (79) has been associating with a younger woman. The couple married fifty-three years ago on St Valentine's Day. Matilde says Rudolph has been seeing his mistress secretly for over forty years. Rudolph says, 'I've had enough.' (*New Zealand Otago Daily Times*)

Italy's Supreme Court has given sex in automobiles its approval, as long as the sex is sufficiently steamy. Ruling on the twelve-year-old appeal of a factory worker and his lady friend, who were given suspended sentences after being caught in his car with their engines going full blast, the court decided that Italian lovers can do what they want in their own cars, as long as the car windows are 'uniformly covered' with condensation – either well steamed up or iced over. Said one High Court official: 'That shouldn't prove any trouble for a thrill-seeking couple who are enjoying themselves.' (*Daily Telegraph*)

An elderly woman who saw a pair of naked legs sticking out of a hedgerow snowdrift thought she had found a murder victim. Emergency calls went out, and a local man led police and ambulancemen to the spot in Nuneaton. Suddenly a couple making love leapt out of the snow and fled across a field clutching their clothes. The girl was completely naked; the man had his socks on. A police

spokesman said, 'They were a couple of cool customers.'
It was minus three degrees centigrade at the time. (Daily
Express)

Several years ago, authorities in Yugoslavia's Vojvodina
province, concerned that some young couples were
rushing into marriage, instituted a mandatory one-month
waiting period for young people intending to marry. And,
in the town of Subotica, at least, the cooling-off period
has been an unrousing success. Officials there say that,
since the one-month wait was instituted, one out of every
two couples has had a change of heart. (*Daily Telegraph*)

Hanover House Industries has a mail order catalogue out
that's aimed at the elderly. Among the items offered is a
book called *Sex After 60*. It's in large type. (*Wall Street
Journal*)

If hints don't work and excuses don't do the trick, Terry
Morgan has a deal for you. 'We take the most difficult
situations in life,' said Morgan, operator of Dump-a-Date
and Kiss-Off-a-Date in Chicago, which feature not so
subtle ways to end relationships. Clients who call Dump-
A-Date are asked to provide all the grisly details they can
on the personality and whims of the recipient. 'Now we
don't want to hurt people,' Morgan said, 'but if you tell
us what the person definitely dislikes, we've got it.'
Terry's terror tactics include the sending of a bunch of
dead flowers, a carton of rotten fruit, and an empty candy
box. (Canadian 'Citizen')

Greece's socialist government has brought in a new law
that legalises civil marriages – in other words, those made
outside the church. But couples will have to speak their
vows in an emphatic manner. In order to guard against
shotgun weddings, the official government regulations

stipulate that the word 'yes' must be spoken in a 'positive and unreserved manner'. (*The Times*)

This personal want ad appeared in the *San Antonio Express*: 'Attractive (some say) widow in her forties wishes to meet companionable gentleman. Must know how to operate lawn mower.' (*New Yorker*)

A scheduled talk at the Camden School for Girls, on why women aren't getting ahead, was postponed because the speaker, leading female political figure Polly Toynbee of the Social Democratic Party, was preoccupied with problems at home. (The Times)

An image-shattering poll by Italy's *Panarama* magazine reveals that nearly 50 per cent of Italian women rate their mates as terrible lovers. Says one observer: 'The news has come as a bombshell to Italian men. Nobody can say what the long-term effects of this disclosure will be, but it is sure to be profound.' (*Los Angeles Herald-Examiner*)

Gwen Hale and Jerry Berdenson of Huntsville, Alabama were determined to get married at the Hamsby's Chapel Methodist Church in rural Morgan County. And they refused to let anything alter their plans, not even a fire that burned the church to the ground. The two tied the knot amid the ashes and rubble. (*Atlanta Journal*)

Her family life didn't work out quite the way she'd planned, says actress Lana Turner. She told TV interviewer Gary Collins: 'My dream was to have one husband and seven children, but instead it turned out the other way.' (Atlanta Journal)

US Congressman Phillip Burton of San Francisco could use some lessons in tailoring one's speeches to the audience being addressed. Speaking to a crowd of gay athletes at the end of the week-long gay athletic games in San Francisco, Burton said: 'I know that for many of you it took genuine courage to be here, but your courage has planted seeds – seeds that will allow your children to grow up free to be who they are.' (Herb Caen, *San Francisco Chronicle*)

Sixty-year-old Jimmy Stevens told a court in the Republic of Vanautu that it was worries about his family that led him to escape from jail, where he was serving a 14½-year sentence for attempting to lead a revolution. Stevens said that he was concerned that there was nobody around to care for his family, and that was a sizeable worry, since he has 23 wives and 48 children. He was sentenced to an extra 2 years and 3 months. (*Daily Telegraph*)

A State Appeals Court in Seattle has turned down Robert J. Irwin's attempt to sue a man, who had sex with his wife, for trespassing. Irwin based his claim on common law provisions dating back to medieval England, which gave a man ownership of his wife's body, and therefore, he maintained, the right to collect monetary damages from anyone who trespasses on his property. However, the court ruled that these provisions are no longer legally viable. (Los Angeles Daily News)

Women's dreams have changed over the last few decades, says Dr Robert van de Castle of the University of Virginia. For one thing, there's more action these days and less talk, and that action includes dreams of outright aggression in which women are the aggressors rather than the passive victims they used to dream of being. Also, he says, women are dreaming less of courtship scenes and weddings, and more about nitty-gritty bedroom activities. (*Los Angeles Herald-Examiner*, 'California Living')

Veronica Parker cannot sue the US Steel Corporation for spousal alienation of affections, just because her now divorced husband fell in love on the job with a fellow US Steel office employee. That's the ruling of Appeals Judge Solie M. Ringold in Seattle. Veronica had maintained that the firm knew or should have known about the romance between her husband James and his present wife, Virginia, and that it was negligent in failing to interfere with the relationship or inform her. The court decided that 'US Steel owed no duty to its employees' spouses to monitor and safeguard their marriages.' (*San Francisco Chronicle*)

The King of Ashanti, in West Africa, is limited by law to 3,333 wives. (Science Digest)

Careless use of the word 'love' spelled doom for the marriage of Giovanni and Maria Condoluco, just two hours after they were wed in Rosarno, Italy. The problem was sparked by a telegram to Maria, read at the wedding feast, which said: 'Congratulations and all happiness. Love, Franco.' As they drove off on their honeymoon, the groom pressed his bride to tell him who this love-guy Franco was. She insisted he was just an old school chum. Disbelieving her, he stopped the car at a bridge and threw her off, then jumped too. She survived. He didn't. Police checked out Franco and confirmed that he was a happily married man who just liked signing his greetings with 'love'. (*Sunday Express*)

Russian doctors are blaming a lack of sex education for what may be the world's highest divorce rate – in the big cities, as many as one out of every two marriages collapses. There are sex manuals in the libraries, but only doctors are allowed to see them. A brave attempt at sex education was made in Leningrad, with the opening of a

Sex Clinic. But, alas, it closed soon after opening, due to what the authorities termed 'embarrassment'. (*Daily Telegraph*)

William Sroka has won a court order in Sault Ste Marie, Ontario, preventing his wife Gertrude from entering his basement study, where he works writing his second novel – he's still looking for a publisher for his first. In seeking judicial relief from Gertrude's intrusions, Sroka told Judge I. A. Vannini that she often rummaged around in the room while he was trying to work , making it hard for him to get his writing done. He admitted that the 24-year-old marriage wasn't in the best of shape, but said 'We're locked in', because of their two teenagers, joint ownership of an apartment building, and the fact that he can't afford a divorce. (Vancouver Sun)

Bad news for construction workers and other like-minded girl-oglers: Dr Melvin Spira, Head of the Plastic Surgery Division of the Baylor College of Medicine in Houston, reports that an increasing number of teenage girls, many as young as 14 or 15, are seeking plastic surgery to reduce the size of their breasts. (*New York Times*)

Students at the University of Philippines Population Institute learn family planning under a 'Miss Concepcion'. Teaching family planning is Miss Mercedes Concepcion. (*The Guardian*)

The Wall Street Journal *reports on a poll which finds that 59 per cent of women think most swimsuits worn by young women are too revealing, but only 33 per cent of men feel this way. Which goes to show that men and women don't always see eye-to-eye.* (Wall Street Journal)

The author of *How to Make Love to A Woman*, which advises men to forget the macho bit and be more sensitive towards women, has been charged in New York with third-degree assault, for breaking a bone in his girlfriend's jaw, as well as a tooth. Michael Morgenstern, a lawyer, allegedly punched 22-year-old Ethel Parks in the face, the day after she moved out of their apartment. Two days earlier, he had returned home unexpectedly to find her with another man. (*Los Angeles Times*)

Congressman Clarence J. Brown, the Republican nominee for Governor of Ohio, has publicly apologised to reporter Mary Ann Sharkey of the *Dayton Journal Herald* for telling her, 'Go into my salon and take off your clothes' when she arrived at his campaign headquarters for an interview. He said he was only playing doctor; he had so many appointments that day, that his staff joked it was like a doctor's office. (*New York Times*)

A woman who placed a lonely hearts ad in the 'Personal' section of a Riga, Russia newspaper, had second thoughts about the attributes she claimed. According to the paper's editor, Voldemar Pupitz, she wrote the paper a letter asking that her ad be changed, explaining 'I wrote "an attractive woman of 34, teetotaller, engineer, seeking friend and father to boy of 11". Now I would ask you most sincerely not to print the words "attractive" and "teetotaller".' (Daily Telegraph)

The Windsor, Ontario newspaper *The Windsor Star* says it will continue to be 'business as usual' for its 'Star Gazers' photo feature. That means that pretty as opposed to not-so-pretty, or downright ugly, women will continue to be featured, despite a ruling by the Ontario Press Council that 'because it features only pretty women' it is 'a form of sex-stereotyping'. The council issued its ruling after receiving complaints about the policy of selecting the gazed-upon women on the basis of their appearance. Objecting were the Windsor Women's Incentive Centre and the Windsor Women Teachers Association (*Vancouver Sun*)

After a few years in which nudist and non-nudist park-goers were rubbing each other up the wrong way in Munich, Germany's Englischer Garten, city officials have passed a law setting up nude and non-nude areas in the 919-acre park. Police Chief Manfred Schreiber says his men will generally look the other way, issuing tickets only in the 'gravest cases' of nudity. (*Newsweek*)

With women increasingly seeking romance with younger men, this news item isn't as surprising as it may have once been, but still it's worth passing on; as hundreds of townsfolk in Omegna, Italy cheered, 19-year-old Fulvio Cerutti married 85-year-old Maria Pia Cerutti. Since the bride owns considerable property, the newlyweds saw fit to dispel any suspicions of financial motives by stating that they would not share their possessions. Said the groom: 'She was living alone in awful conditions. I started helping her and after a time she could do nothing without me. The idea of getting married came to us both simultaneously.' (Seattle Times)

The British hospital periodical *Hospital Doctor/On Call* has been reprimanded by the Press Council for publishing a picture of a naked male corpse that was tattooed from neck to ankle, as a curiosity piece. No effort was made to disguise the face of the man, who had suddenly collapsed and died. But it was obvious that the man had wanted to keep his tattoos a private matter, the Council said, since his wife told police that she hadn't even been aware he was tattooed. (*The Times*)

When a man leaves his sexual partner breathless, it could be that she's allergic to his semen, according to University of Cincinnati allergist, I. Leonard Bernstein. He says the protein coat surrounding sperm cells can provoke, in susceptible women, extreme allergic attacks, like asthma, breathing difficulties or even shock. In the future. Bernstein hopes to develop a desensitising treatment. For now, such women can only have sex when the male partner uses a condom. (*Omni Magazine*)

Under pressure from Evangelical Christians and administrators at California State University in Long Beach, Professor Barry Singer has decided to drop a sex-as-homework option from his 'Psychology of Sex' course. The option had allowed students to fulfil part of their homework requirements by engaging in homosexual, group or premarital sex. The students were required to keep a 'playbook' describing their feelings and practices. Said Singer: 'It can be a very powerful growth and learning experience.' He said that it was common, for example, for heterosexual women to earn their points by trying a lesbian experience. Singer pointed out that his prior permission was required for any such projects, and also that the student's regular sexual partner had to be informed. (Los Angeles Times)

A woman in Luebben, East Germany has divorced her husband because he helped so much around the house, she was left with nothing to do, a West German news agency reports. The woman told the court that the man she at first considered a 'dream of a husband', because of all his cleaning, baby-caring, cooking, shopping and so on, eventually drove her crazy. She said: 'What was left for me to do?' (*San Francisco Chronicle*)

The South Shore Plaza shopping centre in Braintree, Massachusetts has pulled the plug on its electronic Punch and Judy display after a complaint that Punch's violent antics were encouraging wife abuse. The complainer, Ursula Garfield of Bridgewater, a former project director for family planning services, noted: 'This is the season of the year when domestic violence increases.' (*San Francisco Chronicle*)

Newlywed Tim Taylor decided he was too busy with his Bristol toy store to take a honeymoon, so he sent his bride Stephanie off on a five-day honeymoon with her new mother-in-law, his mother, Barbara Taylor. The bride said on returning, 'Tim is rather unromantic'. (Los Angeles Times)

Sex for money has been going the way of the horse and buggy in Chicago, according to police. They've charged 23-year-old Sue Cooper with soliciting for prostitution, the action to be conducted in the back of a horse-drawn carriage, one of many used to conduct leisurely tours of the choice areas of town. The carriage driver, 29-year-old Arthur Tetreault, was charged with keeping a horse of ill repute – that should be house of ill repute. Charges were laid after a detective was quoted a price of $30 for the ride. (*St Louis Post-Dispatch*)

A key advisor to California Governor Jerry Brown, Jacques Barzaghi, was recovering in hospital from a heart attack in Los Angeles when some unfortunate complications occurred. According to *San Francisco Chronicle* columnist Herb Caen, a lady friend came up to see him, identifying herself to nurses as 'Mrs Barzaghi'. She was followed almost immediately by Mrs Barzaghi. The conversation between the two ladies was not what doctors recommend in those circumstances. (Herb Caen, *San Francisco Chronicle*)

An Eldora, Iowa farmer desperate to win back his estranged girlfriend paid $7,500 to a psychic he found through a newspaper ad, say authorities in Des Moines. She advised him to rub himself with a tomato and then place the tomato under his pillow. Alas, it didn't work, and he was left as crushed as his tomato. Authorities would like to lay charges if they can find any that apply. (Portland Oregonian)

Newlyweds George and Jane Kay of Flamborough, Yorkshire hardly had a chance to enjoy their wedding gifts before dustmen hauled them all away. They had put all the gifts in their fenced yard while they redecorated their house. Now they're consulting a lawyer, after East Yorkshire Borough Council refused them any compensation for the lawnmower, cutlery, crockery, glasses and pans. Says a Council spokesman: 'Our men had no reason to believe that these materials were anything but rubbish.' (*Daily Telegraph*)

There are sex manuals galore, but now Los Angeles lawyer Merle H. Horowitz has come out with a manual dealing with what for many lovers is a taboo subject, who gets what when they split up. No bedside should be without Horowitz's 44-page book called *Love is Love, but Business is Business*. It includes tear-out contracts covering areas like leases, child support, property, debts, living expenses and season tickets. Send $10 plus postage and handling to Hillimer and Associates, 2029 Century Park East, Suite 1850, L.A.90067. (*Los Angeles Daily News*)

They had been married to each other and divorced once before but, in Great Bend, Kansas, Herman Cofer and Irene Ernst decided to give it another whirl, thirty-seven years after their previous fifteen-year hook-up ended. Says the new Mrs Cofer: 'I think it was best that he wasn't ready for me back then.' Now that they're both in their seventies, they think they have the maturity to make it work. Both have had two other marriages since their last one ended. (Sacramento Bee)

Marital bliss was short-lived for 20-year-old Alan Locke and his French-born bride Bridget, a London divorce court was told. Five minutes after they were joined together at a registry office, the bride said she had to make a phone call, and said Locke, 'She went off and never came back.' After searching high and low for her, he finally traced her to a Paris address but, he said, 'She slammed the door in my face.' Locke said they had known each other for a year before their marriage, but some things you don't find out until after the knot is tied. (*Daily Telegraph*)

A church organist has been fired for trading in his old organs for a new set. Organist Dr Nigel Gee had to face the music from the vicar at St Nicholas' Parish Church in Wallasey, Cheshire, when he showed up as Dr Helen Gee, after a successful sex-change operation. Mrs Gee – that's Nigel's wife, obtained a divorce and moved out with their three sons. All inquiries on the matter have been referred by church officials to the Bishop of Chester, but callers were told that the Bishop is now abroad. (*Daily Telegraph*)

Pericles Alfonsos had to serve three months in prison, after he had his father-in-law over for a dinner of duck which he said he had just shot. The Athens man was

*always heading off for a day or two of hunting, and
returning with meat for the table. However, at that fateful
duck dinner, his wife's father developed the sneaking
suspicion that the duck was actually frozen, not fresh.
Suspecting fowl play, the wife and her father trailed
Alfonsos on his next hunting trip. The trail ended at the
door of his girlfriend's apartment. So that was the game
he was bagging. Alfonsos has now been sentenced to three
months in prison for adultery.* (Daily Telegraph)

Somebody in Miami must have taken to heart recent
reports that jogging whets the sexual appetite. An
unidentified man told police that he was kidnapped while
out on his customary twenty-mile run. He said he had a
bag tossed over his head, and then was taken to a house
where a woman raped him. He was then dumped in a
field in what police called a 'very hysterical and
traumatised state'. (*Jet Magazine*)

Doreen Learmont's patience with her slow-to-warm
husband ran out after twenty-one years of marriage. A
court granted Doreen, 55, a divorce from 60-year-old
Clifford Learmont, of North Walsham, Norfolk, after
hearing that, after twenty-one years together, he still
hadn't got around to having sex with her. She finally grew
fed up with waiting. (*Daily Telegraph*)

*A Munich, West Germany woman has been sentenced to
six months in jail in Salonica, Greece, for touring the
country in a mobile home which she converted into a
mobile brothel. Forty-year-old Helen Corbel was arrested
outside the student residence halls of Salonica University,
after lecturers there complained to police about the
number of lectures she was causing students to miss.*
(Daily Telegraph)

According to a survey of distance runners by the magazine *The Runner*, 26.5 per cent say they would give up sex before they would quit running. Among women, the figure was 38.1 per cent. (*Los Angeles Daily News*)

Students on a New York University Human Sexuality Course will have the chance to get abroad this summer for some first-hand fieldwork in Sri Lanka. According to the course outline it offers: 'An in-depth examination of the sexual customs, beliefs and mores of Sri Lanka. Cross-cultural comparisons with American sexuality are made through field trips, excursions, guest speakers, interaction with Sri Lanka professionals, groups, and with an experiential educational methodology.' (*New Yorker*)

A woman who bared her grievances in an all-night grocery store by removing her bathing suit to protest against high apartment rents can get it back from police in the mountain resort town of Ruidoso, New Mexico. Police have the bathing suit hanging on a wall at their station, and the woman can have it if she tries it on to prove it fits. Store manager Bob Smith says the disgruntled woman who seemed to be in her thirties, entered the store about 4.15 a.m. and began screaming about high apartment rents. To emphasise her points, she removed the bathing suit she was wearing and exited into the freezing night in white panties that Smith described as 'very brief, very brief'. (*St Louis Post-Dispatch*)

Old age is the time when most people could be enjoying the best sexual experiences of their lives, says Dr Cathleen Cairns, a sex therapist and Professor of Counselling Psychology at the University of Calgary, Alberta. 'Their sexual contact can become more sensual,' she says, once men start having problems achieving orgasm. That can

135

free them to use their imagination in finding new ways to satisfy their mate. (Toronto Globe & Mail)

For one single San Diego woman, turning 31 hasn't been marked by worries about when the marriage offers will start rolling in. In fact, since her 31st birthday on 11 March, Angela de Palo has received at least twenty-four serious offers of marriage. Maybe it has something to do with the fact that she learned on her birthday that she had won $1,000 a week for life in Kodak's 'Set for Life' sweepstakes. She says suitors 'tell me they think I'm a nice person . . . that they can tell I'm family-oriented'. De Palo hasn't met any of her suitors and says she has no intention of meeting any of them. (*San Diego Union*)

So you think Japanese companies have the ideal system of labour-relations? According to James W. Begun, Assistant Professor at Cornell's University Graduate Business School, Japanese workers have a derogatory term for employees who put their family ahead of the company. They're called 'wife-lovers'. (*Christian Science Monitor*)

William and Flossie Wellman and their four children have filed a $6 million lawsuit in Los Angeles Superior Court against Glamour *magazine, which used a photograph of the family to illustrate an article about incest. The family said that the photo was obtained from a filing company and used without their permission, conveying an impression of family togetherness that was unwarranted.* (Los Angeles Daily News)

The newly crowned Mrs America, Rhonda McGeeney, is an ideal representative of the modern American wife, says her proud husband Patrick McGeeney, a Houston advertising executive. That's because, at age 29, Rhonda is already on her third husband. Said the new Mrs America:

'Divorce is a decision many women have faced or will have to face, and I hope to inspire them to be able to face the darkness.' (*Los Angeles Times*)

At least eighteen women in San José, California have now told police that they have received middle-of-the-night calls from a man who is being dubbed 'The Silver-Tongued Telephone Seducer'. The seducer solicits sex from divorcees by pretending to be their ex-husband. His method of operation is to phone a divorcee around 3 a.m. and identify himself as her ex. He explains that his voice sounds different because he has a cold. He says he'd like to give marriage another whirl, but first she has to sleep with a friend of his. If the woman agrees, the man then shows up as the friend. Understandably this line doesn't work with everyone, but San José police say that at least three women have fallen for it and had sex with the stranger, who is described as having 'sort of a football image with a bit of a gut'. Police aren't sure how he gets divorcees' phone numbers, but speculate that he makes hundreds of calls before reaching a divorced woman who actually wants her husband back. (*San Francisco Chronicle*)

A new law passed by Sweden's Parliament permits husbands to take their wife's surname if they wish. Or, the marriage partners can have different surnames, in which case they have to decide on their children's surnames. If they don't notify officials of that choice within three months of a child's birth, then the child, naturally, will assume the mother's surname. (San Franciso Chronicle)

A memo from the management division of Britain's Civil Service, on the subject of secretary-sharing, suggests: 'This can be done either horizontally between officers of equal rank, or vertically between an officer and a senior.' (*Chicago Tribune*)